SPECIAL OCCASIONS

SPECIAL OCCASIONS

*

THE BEST OF MARTHA STEWART LIVING

Originally published in book form by Time Warner in 1994. Published simultaneously by Clarkson N. Potter, Oxmoor House, Inc., and Leisure Arts.

The recipes and photographs in this work were previously published in Martha Stewart Living.

Manufactured in the United States of America.

Library of Congress Catalog Number: 94-68056 (hardcover)

94-68056 (paperback)

ISBN: 0-8487-1430-X (hardcover)

0-8487-1478-4 (paperback)

Endpaper design: Czechoslovakian polished linen damask (1910-1920) from the Vito Giallo Collection, New York City.

Edited by Isolde Motley and Amy Schuler

Design associates: Francesca Richer
Domitilla Sartogo
Pui Kuen Wan

Typesetting and composition by Terence Wight

Book design by Yolanda Cuomo, NYC

ACKNOWLEDGMENTS

Many, many people have contributed to the issues of MARTHA STEWART LIVING from which this book is drawn.

At the magazine itself: Eric Thorkilsen, David Steward, Gael Towey, Susan Wyland, Peter Mark, Sarah Medford, Linda Nardi, Lisa Wagner, Laura Harrigan, Wayne Wolf, Tamara Westmark, Susan Spungen, Hannah Milman, Eugenia Leftwich, Lauren Stanich, Laurel Reed Caputo, Eric Pike, Wanda Lau, Celia Barbour, Anne Johnson, Darcy Miller, Dora Braschi Cardinale, Marc Einsele, Heidi Posner, Carole Rogers, Frances Boswell, Claudia Bruno, and Page Marchese.

At Martha's home and in her Westport office: Renato and Renaldo Abreu, Rita Christiansen, Necy Fernandes, Carolyn Kelly, Marie Mendez, Judy Morris, Kathleen Oberman, Laura Herbert Plimpton, and Alexis Stewart.

At Oxmoor House, in Birmingham, Alabama: Bruce Akin, Nancy Fitzpatrick, Marianne Jordan, Phillip Lee, John McIntosh, and Gail Morris. At Satellite Graphics, in New York City, Ernest V. Cardinale, and at Quebecor Printing, in Kingsport, Tennessee, Myra Tiller.

For their inspiration and support: A.C. Barnett, Anita Calero, Jaimie Epstein, Annmarie Iverson, Fritz Karch, Allen Lacy, Bo Niles, Andrea Raisfeld, Margaret Roach, Steve Rubin, Merrill Shindler, Deborah Smith, and Katherine Whiteside.

CONTENTS

1 new year's day
soup buffet & winter blossoms

Flaky Parmesan Crackers 16 Grissini 17 Fish Soup 18 Fish Stock 18 Rouille 18 Fresh Pea Soup 20 Chicken Stock 20 Roasted Vegetable Soup 21 Caramelized Lemon Tart 22 Pâte Sucrée 22

2 valentine's day
romantic dinner & chocolate

Gougères 28 Heart Salad 29 Coq au Champagne 30 Roasted Pepper Hearts with Parsnip Puree 30 Vegetable Hearts 31 Rich Chocolate Soufflé 33 Chocolate Romance 34 Chocolate Ganache 34

3 easter sunday
spring breakfast

Buttermilk French Toast 40 Warm Berry Compote 40 Bloody Marys 40 Poached Eggs on Rounds of Polenta 42 Blanched Asparagus 43 Herb Beurre Blanc 43

4 a fine spring day
salads & growing greens

Spring Salad with Citrus Vinaigrette 46 Caesar Salad 46 Herbed Tomato Salad 47 Grilled Shiitake Mushrooms on Japanese Greens 49 Mesclun Salad 49 Pencil Asparagus with Tarragon Oil 49 Yellow Tomato Vinaigrette 49 Frisée with Sautéed Shrimp, Marinated Olives, and Capers 50

5 mother's day
ladies' luncheon & decorating cakes

Consommé with Herb Dumplings 56 Chicken Stock 57 Herb Dumplings 57 Navarin of Lamb with Spring Vegetables 58 Mashed Potatoes with Sorrel 58 Pansy Layer Cake 60 Angel Food Sheet Cake 60 Meringues 61 Vanilla Buttercream 61 Coconut Cloud 63 Seven-Minute Icing 63 Raspberry Ruffle 64 Raspberry Syrup 64 Meringue Buttercream 64

6 graduation day
garden party

Pearl Balls 70 Vegetable Dumplings 71 Spicy Dipping Sauce 71 Seafood Dumplings 71 Fillet of Beef Balsamico with Red Onion Confit 72 Red Onion Confit 72 Roasted Red Pepper Dip 72 Mussels Remoulade 74 Remoulade Sauce 75 Cold Sesame Noodles 75

7 first day of summer
tuscan feast & poppy bouquets

Grilled Mushrooms, Fennel, and Peppers 80 Grilled Swiss Chard Packets 81 Torta di Riso 83 Grilled Shrimp in the Shells 83 Granita di Caffé 84 Baked Stuffed Peaches 84

8 a wedding at home
tea party

Meringue Mushrooms 93 Carpaccio Teardrops 93 Basil Aïoli 93 Violet Nosegays 94 Asparagus with Basil Tarragon Dipping Sauce 95 Smoked Salmon Roses 95 Lemon Crème Fraîche 95 Cream Scones 95 Praline Calla Lilies with Lemon Cream 96 Blueberry Pinwheels 96

9 fourth of july
a classic picnic

Spicy Fried Chicken 102 Stars and Stripes Salad 103 Peanut Coleslaw 104 Old-Fashioned Blueberry Pie 104 Pâte Brisée 105

10 midsummer
supper on the beach & outdoor lighting

White Gazpacho with Grapes 108 White Sangria 108 Paella 111 Grill Roasted Vegetables 112 Aïoli 112 Flan 112

11 labor day weekend
tastes of provence

Deviled Crayfish 118 Pistou Soup 121 Country Leg of Lamb 124 Apple Tart 124

12 all hallow's eve
potluck supper & carving pumpkins

Cold Seafood Salad 130 Shallot and Artichoke Tarts 131 Mark Peel's Pesto 131 Braised Veal Shanks 132 Salsa Verde 132 Pear Bread Pudding 134

INTRODUCTION

1994 was an important year in our family's history. My mother, Martha Kostyra, celebrated her eightieth birthday on September 16, 1994, and we, her six children, gave her a party on September 18. Months before the actual birthday we started to confer about what we could do to make this occasion special. We decided that we should ask Mom what she had thought about, and dreamed about. She answered simply, "I want a bash. A bash with all my friends and family that everyone will remember."

Who to invite? Ask Mother. She came up with a wonderful list of approximately one hundred guests, her dream list. My office sent out a postcard announcing the date and occasion and asking her guests to save the date, invitation to follow.

More conferring. Where to have the party? Ask Mother. She insisted that it be at the Fairfield County Hunt Club, neutral ground, where no one of us would be burdened with a large gathering at our home during the very busy back-to-school season.

The six children met over the phone and in person, deciding upon the division of duties and the various obligations involved. We agreed that mother's involvement now would be reduced to showing up at her own party. We all freed our calendars and started in earnest designing the invitation, the menu, and the entertainment. Because of my graphics background I undertook the invitation design. It was my sister Laura's idea to use Mother's wedding portrait, a beautiful tinted photograph of Mom at the time she married our father in 1938. Very few of the invited guests had seen this picture and they were so pleased to see her in her rust-colored velvet gown, her hair stylishly wrapped in a gold kerchief. A local stationer printed the invitation and suggested, at added expense, a tissue-lined envelope that greatly enhanced the look of the card. One month before the event the invitations were addressed and mailed by another sister, Kathy, with my office accepting R.S.V.P.s.

Laura and sister-in-law Rita planned the menu with the hunt club (the food was delicious). Maria Calise, who had made Laura's wedding cake, was enlisted to bake and decorate the tiered yellow pound cake with black-currant

filling. Our friend Toni Elling sent two big boxes of sugared pansies; these covered the tiers, cascading down in a beautiful pastel landscape. Laura, the family musician, hired her son's piano teacher, Chris Coogan, to play the Steinway at the club during the party. She also enlisted her son Christopher to play his viola for us before dessert, accompanied by his teacher. Later the two sat down at the piano and played duets, to the great pleasure of Grandmother and the rest of the guests.

My brothers Eric and George manned a video camera during the entire event in hopes of providing all of us with an edited tape of the party. We all agreed that the photographs and the video would be an important memoir for all the grandchildren. Everyone who took photos was asked to send the negatives to us so that Kathy could prepare an album for each of the six children.

Toward the end of the party, we came to its highlight. Starting with Eric, the oldest, each child toasted Mom—declaring that she was always uncompromisingly fair, always "there" when we needed her, and always able to divide her time so that none of us felt left out or ignored. When we were finished with our heartfelt toasts, Mother stood up and gave her toast to all of us, declaring in a strong and happy voice that "the longer we live, the longer we live." This statement was backed up by some serious actuarial research she had done using statistics from articles she had collected. Ending, she invited everyone to return for her ninetieth birthday bash. In short, she made our toasts appear nostalgic and almost "sappy" while she, strong despite her years, was fully in command.

Everyone was amused and thrilled that our schoolteacher mother was still the schoolteacher. What this specially planned "special occasion" accomplished was fantastic. Mother has been on a "high" and more energetic than ever. She seems to have become younger in the days since her party, not older. All of us were able to gather amongst infrequently seen family and guests, some of whom traveled many miles to attend the festivities. We will all remember fondly the embraces and the smiles, and the good time had by all. We will remember the beautiful children who call Mother Grandma or Granny or Mrs. Kostyra. We'll remember Miss Weyer, my mother's eighty-three-year-old friend from New Jersey, who taught me third grade. We'll remember Eric's toast when, after all these years, he intimated that perhaps he was responsible for the family. Our parents had eloped before the real wedding and Mother was actually pregnant when she had the formal ceremony.

What this party became was what we had hoped during its planning. A time for cheerful, gracious, and thought-provoking celebration. It was truly a "special occasion."

Martha Stewart

new year's day

soup buffet
& winter blossoms

flaky parmesan crackers
grissini
fish soup
rouille
fresh pea soup
roasted vegetable soup
caramelized lemon tart

} 1

DELICATE BRANCHES OF
white forsythia (actually not
forsythia at all, but *Abeliophyl-*
lum distichum) have been
forced into bloom. Finding
branches with buds to force is
difficult this early in the
season—but they are worth
searching out.

HOMEMADE CRACKERS *flavored with cheese and spices.*

FLAKY PARMESAN CRACKERS

"Turning" the dough several times gives these crackers their flaky, layered texture. They can also be made with cheddar.

TO MAKE ABOUT 40

1½ cups unbleached all-purpose flour

1 teaspoon salt

½ teaspoon cayenne pepper

8 tablespoons (1 stick) cold unsalted butter, cut into pieces

1½ cups grated Parmesan

2 large egg yolks, mixed with 2 tablespoons cold water

1. Combine flour, salt, and cayenne pepper in a food processor. Add butter and process until mixture resembles coarse meal. Add cheese and combine. Add egg mixture with machine running. Process just until a dough is formed. (Do not overmix.) Gather into a flattened ball, wrap in plastic, and chill for 1 hour.

3. Heat oven to 350°. Divide dough in half. Roll one of the halves into a rectangle ¼ inch thick. Fold into thirds and rotate a quarter turn. Roll, fold, and rotate two more times, finishing with dough folded into thirds. Repeat procedure with second piece of dough.

4. Roll out dough to ⅛ inch thick. Cut into decorative shapes. Prick each cracker several times with a fork, and bake on ungreased baking sheets for 20 minutes, turning after 10 to 15 minutes. Cool on wire racks.

GRISSINI

These Italian-style breadsticks can be enjoyed soft, fresh from the oven, but will become crunchy as they cool.

TO MAKE 24

1¾ teaspoons active dry yeast

  Pinch of sugar

 ¼ cup warm water

1½ cups cold water

 3 tablespoons olive oil, plus more for brushing dough

 4 cups unbleached all-purpose flour

1½ teaspoons salt

  Sesame seeds, poppy seeds, or coarse salt, for sprinkling

1. In a small bowl, combine yeast, sugar, and warm water. Let stand until foamy, about 10 minutes.

2. Combine cold water and olive oil. Combine flour and salt in a food processor. With machine running, pour in yeast mixture followed by water-oil mixture. Mix until dough forms a ball, then process 45 seconds more.

3. Turn out dough onto a lightly floured surface, and finish kneading by hand until soft, smooth, and elastic. Knead in additional flour if the dough is sticky.

4. Divide dough in half. On two lightly oiled cookie sheets, shape dough into two rectangles measuring approximately 8-by-4-by-½ inches. Brush with oil, cover with plastic, and let rise until doubled in bulk, about 1 hour.

5. Heat oven to 375°. Sprinkle dough with seeds or salt, then cut each rectangle widthwise into 12 pieces. Lightly oil another cookie sheet. Pick up each piece of dough by the ends and stretch to about 12 inches, or the length of your cookie sheet. Place sticks about 2 inches apart on sheets, and bake for 15 to 20 minutes, until light brown. They will keep for several days stored in an airtight container.

{ Homemade crackers

Restaurant critics often admit to a simple rule of thumb: if the bread or crackers are good, the rest of the meal will follow. Guests at your party can feel the same way: a heap of freshly baked crackers or a loaf of warm bread tell them that you have paid attention to every detail of the meal.

Consider the flavors and textures of the soup, and choose a complementary cracker, or tailor a recipe. Our grissini (readied for baking, below) were flavored with sesame seeds, poppy seeds, and coarse salt, but you might try celery seeds, rosemary, or sweet-red-pepper flakes. You can also experiment with shape—once you have the dough in hand, breadsticks can be initials to identify a guest's place, flat crackers can be shaped with cutters into hearts, stars, or even dinosaurs for a child's party.

FISH SOUP

Once you prepare all the ingredients, this soup is easy to make.

TO SERVE 4

2 cloves garlic, thinly sliced

3 tablespoons olive oil

1 medium onion, finely diced

2 carrots, finely diced

1 stalk celery, finely diced

½ bulb fresh fennel, thinly sliced

1 tablespoon tomato paste

Pinch of saffron

1 bay leaf

¼ cup chopped flat-leaf parsley

Salt and freshly ground pepper

2 cups dry white wine

32 pieces assorted shellfish, such as mussels, clams, and live
scallops, well scrubbed; mussels debearded

2 cups canned plum tomatoes, drained and pureed

1 cup peeled, seeded, and chopped fresh tomatoes

2 cups Fish Stock (recipe follows)

1 pound monkfish, membrane removed

½ pound red snapper fillets, skin on

½ pound medium shrimp, peeled and deveined

1. In a large, wide pot over low heat, cook garlic in olive oil until
golden brown. Add onion, carrots, celery, and fennel, and cook
until soft, about 10 minutes. Stir in tomato paste. Add saffron,
bay leaf, and 1 tablespoon of the parsley. Season lightly with salt
and pepper. Cook a few minutes more.

2. Stir in wine and add shellfish. Cover pot; steam until shells
open, about 5 minutes. Discard unopened shells.

3. Add tomatoes and stock. Bring to a boil, then reduce heat and
simmer for 10 minutes over medium-high heat.

4. Rinse fish and cut into 2-inch pieces. Add to pot along with
shrimp. Lower heat, cover pot, and cook gently until fish is cooked
through, 5 to 10 minutes. Adjust seasonings; stir in remaining
chopped parsley, reserving some for garnish.

5. Divide seafood among four large bowls, ladle broth over top,
garnish with parsley, and serve with Rouille (recipe follows).

FISH STOCK

TO MAKE 1 QUART

1 tablespoon olive oil

1 carrot, chopped

1 onion, finely chopped

1 stalk celery, finely chopped

1 small piece fennel, chopped

2 pounds fish heads and bones, gills removed, from nonoily
whitefish such as red snapper, sole, or flounder, rinsed well

2 cups dry white wine

1 tomato, cut into pieces

1 bay leaf

Parsley sprigs

10 peppercorns

3 cups water, or to cover

1. Heat oil in a large pot. Add vegetables and cook until slightly
soft, about 5 minutes. Add fish heads and bones, and cook until
they turn white and opaque, about 5 minutes.

2. Add remaining ingredients and bring to a boil. Lower heat to
medium and cook for 20 minutes. Skim off any foam.

3. Strain through a fine mesh strainer lined with cheesecloth. To
store, let cool, then freeze in small containers for future use.

ROUILLE

Stir this fiery sauce into Fish Soup.

TO MAKE ABOUT ¾ CUP

1 red pepper

3 small dried chili peppers, seeded and soaked in hot water

2 cloves garlic

1 2-inch slice French bread, crust removed, soaked in water
and squeezed dry

2 tablespoons olive oil

¼ cup hot Fish Stock or Fish Soup broth

Salt

1. Roast pepper over gas flame or under broiler until blackened.
Place in paper bag to cool; peel and seed.

2. In a blender, puree peppers, garlic, and bread. Slowly add oil
with blender running, and mix until smooth. Add stock or broth,
and blend until smooth; season with salt. Serve immediately.

CLASSIC FISH SOUP, with mussels and clams still in their shells and a bowl of rouille (spicy mayonnaise) served on the side.

f RESH PEA SOUP

The bright flavor of this simple soup is best the day that it's made.

TO SERVE 8

    2 tablespoons olive oil

    3 large scallions, white part only, finely chopped

    1 large yellow onion, finely chopped

    2 celery stalks, finely diced

    Salt and freshly ground pepper

    4 cups Chicken Stock (recipe follows)

    5 cups fresh peas, about 4 to 5 pounds unshelled

1. In a large pot, combine olive oil, scallions, onion, celery, and salt and pepper. Cook partially covered over low heat for 1 hour or until vegetables are very soft, stirring often.

2. Add stock and bring to a simmer. Stir in 4 cups of the peas, and bring to a boil. Cook just until peas are hot, about 5 minutes.

3. Let cool slightly, about 15 minutes. Puree soup in small batches in a blender. Place soup in a clean pot, and return to a simmer.

4. Blanch remaining 1 cup peas and use as garnish for each bowl.

CHICKEN STOCK

Freeze in small containers and defrost only as much as you need.

TO MAKE 2 TO 3 QUARTS

    2 3-pound chickens, cut up

    2 onions, peeled and quartered

    2 celery stalks, cut into 2-inch pieces

    2 carrots, cut into 2-inch pieces

    1 leek, washed and cut up

    2 bay leaves

    Parsley sprigs

    Several sprigs fresh herbs, such as thyme or rosemary

  10 peppercorns

    4 quarts water

1. Place all ingredients in a large stockpot. Bring slowly to a boil, skimming foam often. Reduce heat and simmer for 4 to 5 hours, skimming occasionally. Do not allow stock to boil.

2. Strain stock through a fine mesh strainer lined with cheesecloth. Discard solids. Refrigerate overnight and remove fat.

Roasted-vegetable soup is garnished with fresh basil.

Whole peas add texture to a pureed fresh pea soup.

candle-lit chandelier and Kent Irish linen in oyster and celadon set the mood.

ROASTED VEGETABLE SOUP

This soup can be eaten the day it's made, but the flavor improves if you let it sit overnight.

TO SERVE 8

  2 medium eggplants
  2 small yellow onions
  1 head garlic
  1 large tomato
  2 red peppers
  2 tablespoons olive oil
 20 fresh basil leaves
    Sprig of fresh oregano
    Salt and freshly ground pepper
3-4 cups Chicken Stock (see page 20)
  1 cup freshly grated Parmesan
  2 tablespoons unsalted butter

1. Heat oven to 350°. Prick eggplants several times with a fork, and place on a cookie sheet. Place unpeeled onions, unpeeled garlic, and tomato on another cookie sheet. Roast for about 1 hour, until very soft. (Remove tomato after 30 minutes.) Place in a bowl to cool.

2. Roast peppers directly over a gas flame until skin is black. Let steam in a brown paper bag until cool. Peel and seed peppers and set aside.

3. When cool enough to handle, peel eggplants; cut in half, and remove and discard strips of seeds from the centers. Peel tomato and squeeze out seeds. Peel onions and cut into large pieces. Slice head of garlic about ½ inch from top and squeeze out roasted cloves.

4. In a large pot, heat olive oil. Add vegetables, garlic, 10 whole basil leaves, and the leaves of the oregano sprig. Season with salt and pepper. Cook for about 30 minutes, stirring often.

5. Add 3 cups stock; simmer for 30 minutes.

6. Let cool slightly, about 15 minutes. Puree soup in batches in a blender. (Do not fill blender more than half full.) Place soup in a clean pot, and return to a simmer. Thin with additional stock, if needed, to reach desired consistency. Stir in cheese and cook over low heat, stirring, until melted, about 10 minutes. Before serving, stir in butter; adjust seasonings.

7. Shred remaining basil leaves and use as garnish for each bowl.

CARAMELIZED LEMON TART

Lemon tarts are seasonless, and always provide a refreshing note.

TO MAKE ONE 12-INCH TART

  2 cups sugar

  1 cup fresh lemon juice, strained

  12 large egg yolks

   Zest of 2 lemons

  ½ pound (2 sticks) unsalted butter, cut into pieces

  1 Pâte Sucrée tart shell (recipe follows), baked and cooled

   Sugar for caramelizing top

1. Place sugar and lemon juice in a large stainless-steel bowl. Push yolks through a sieve into bowl, and whisk to combine.

2. Set bowl over a pot of simmering water, and whisk until mixture thickens, 15 to 20 minutes. Cook 5 minutes longer.

3. Remove bowl from heat, and stir in zest. Stir in butter piece by piece until completely melted. Pour into tart shell; chill until firm.

4. Preheat broiler. Remove outer ring from tart pan and place pan on a large baking sheet. Sift sugar evenly over top, and place under broiler. Remove tart when top is evenly browned.

PÂTE SUCRÉE

TO MAKE ONE 12-INCH TART SHELL

2½ cups all-purpose flour

  3 tablespoons sugar

 ½ pound (2 sticks) cold unsalted butter, cut into pieces

  2 large egg yolks beaten with 4 tablespoons ice water

1. Combine flour and sugar in a medium bowl. Cut in butter with a pastry blender until mixture resembles coarse meal.

2. Drizzle egg mixture into flour-butter mixture while stirring with a fork. As soon as pastry starts to hold together, stop adding liquid. Shape dough into a flat round, wrap, and chill for at least 1 hour.

3. Heat oven to 375°. Remove dough from refrigerator. On a lightly floured surface, roll out to ⅛ inch thick. Press pastry into tart pan. Run a rolling pin across top to trim. Carefully line pastry with aluminum foil, and weight with beans. Bake for 10 to 15 minutes. When pastry begins to color around edges, remove weights and foil; continue to bake until pastry turns amber, 10 to 12 more minutes. Cool pan on a wire rack completely before filling.

A LEMON TART is presented on an enamelware kitchen tray from the forties. The pie server is heavily engraved American silver, the dessert forks turn-of-the-century Christofle silver, the dessert plate French creamware.

•forcing branches

Coaxing winter branches to blossom before their time is simple: all you have to do is bring the branches indoors and provide them with all the warmth and water they expect from spring.

The easiest branches to force are early-season bloomers (quince, shad, witch hazel), but nearly any will do, as will catkins and leaves. You can gather specimens to experiment with on a walk in the woods, but often you don't have to look farther than your own backyard: try snips of all your shrubs. Apple, cherry, quince, forsythia, spicebush, huckleberry, and other branches that bear small flowers may be cut early, while those that bear large ones should be left outside on their shrubs until the buds are well developed. When you cut branches from fruit trees, be sure to get the fat, wrinkly flowering buds rather than the smooth, pointy vegetative buds, which will produce only leaves.

Once you've collected your branches, cut the ends on a slant with sharp shears and immediately plunge the bare twig into tepid water. Bring them into the coolest spot in the house, or the warmest on the porch: fifty-eight degrees is the ideal temperature for forcing. While you're waiting for the flowers to pop, which may take a week to a month, keep the water in the vases clean and high, mist the branches periodically, and recut the ends whenever they are exposed to the air. Once blossoms appear, make a note of the most fruitful species so you can repeat the performance next year.

{ Branches to force

Because we wanted to try many more types of branches than we had available ourselves, we swapped branches with friends and asked our favorite local tree expert (5) if he could help us out. He came through with a truckload of water-filled plastic buckets bursting with fruit-tree prunings and unusual woodland cuttings. We were successful with everything we tried except lilac (apparently the lilacs available in florists' shops are not really forced but are shipped from warmer places where they're naturally blooming.) What follows is a partial list of branches you can force.

Crab apple *and* beech *(1)*

White forsythia *and* magnolia *(2)*

Apple *(before, 6, and after, 3)*

Highbush huckleberry *(4)*

Pussy willow catkins *(7, with roots sprouting after blooms have faded)*

Quince, forsythia, *and* birch *(8, with* crab apple*)*

Cherry *and* spicebush *(9, pink and green-yellow, respectively; the lilacs in foreground came from a flower market, the others are "mystery twigs")*

And then there's…

Currant

Dogwood

Gooseberry

Mock orange

Moosewood

Pear

Pieris

Privet

Red maple

Shad

Weeping willow

Winter sweet

Witch hazel

valentine's day

romantic dinner

& chocolate

gougères

roasted pepper hearts
with
parsnip puree

coq au champagne

vegetable hearts

heart salad

rich chocolate soufflé

chocolate romance cake

} 2

CHOCOLATE MOLDS were
once made of tin; today
they're usually plastic. But
whether they're old or
new (ours were a mix of both)
make sure they're clean.
Brush chocolate on to ensure
a complete impression
without bubbles.

SAVORY CHEESE PUFFS *on an 1820s Wedgwood plate.*

GOUGÈRES

Gougères are pâte à choux puffs with cheese added to the batter.

TO MAKE ABOUT 50 PUFFS

½ cup all-purpose flour

¾ teaspoon salt

¾ teaspoon freshly ground pepper

1 teaspoon dried thyme

   Pinch of cayenne pepper

1 cup milk

8 tablespoons (1 stick) unsalted butter

4 large eggs, at room temperature

½ cup grated Parmesan

½ cup grated Gruyère

   Egg wash made from 1 large egg and 1 teaspoon water

1. Heat oven to 400°. Sift together flour, salt, pepper, thyme, and cayenne.

2. In a large heavy saucepan over high heat, combine milk and butter, in pieces. Remove from heat the moment it boils; add flour mixture all at once. Stir briskly until mixture pulls away from sides of pan. Return to low heat and beat for half a minute. Remove and let cool slightly.

3. Beat in eggs one at a time until mixture is smooth and just holds its shape. Add cheeses; stir well.

4. Pipe from a pastry bag fitted with a large star tip onto a buttered baking sheet. Brush tops of puffs sparingly with egg wash.

5. Bake for 20 minutes and serve.

HEART SALAD

The truffle oil lends an earthy aroma and flavor to this warm salad.

TO SERVE 2

    4 baby artichokes

    2 lemons, cut in half

1½ tablespoons olive oil
    Salt

 ½ cup chicken stock

    1 tablespoon sherry vinegar
    Freshly ground pepper

    3 tablespoons white-truffle oil

    2 handfuls assorted baby lettuces (we
      used lollo rossa, red oak, red romaine)

    2 pieces heart of palm, sliced at an angle
      Chervil or parsley leaves, for garnish

1. Pull off tough outer artichoke leaves. Peel stems and trim bottoms; trim about ¼ inch from tops. Cut artichokes in half lengthwise and put in a bowl of cold water. Squeeze lemons into bowl; add rinds, and soak for 20 minutes.

2. Heat olive oil in a small sauté pan; add drained artichokes cut side down. Cook over medium heat until well browned, about 5 minutes. Turn over, sprinkle with salt, add chicken stock, and bring to a boil. Reduce heat and simmer until tender, 5 to 10 minutes. Discard excess stock; keep artichokes warm.

3. Whisk together vinegar, salt, and pepper. Slowly whisk in truffle oil. Toss lettuces with all but 1 tablespoon of dressing. Divide greens between plates and top with artichokes and hearts of palm. Drizzle remaining dressing over top. Garnish with herbs and serve.

{ Vintage linen

The napkins on the Valentine's table are old damask, found in a tag-sale bundle. Vintage linens like these are still affordable, and unlike other collectibles, they can be put to daily use. True antiques are rare; most of the linens one finds are Victorian, Edwardian, or of later date. To buy, go to tag sales, flea markets, consignment shops, and antiques shops. If you find an interesting piece of fabric, open it up. Don't worry if it looks yellowed, just put it to soak in nonchlorine bleach, greatly diluted, until it appears white. Stains are another matter: it's hard to remove unidentifiable fifty-year-old marks or the brown spots of oxidation. Hold the fabric up to the light to see if there are repairs or thin spots. Crumple a bit to see if the fibers are brittle—that's incurable.

Monogramming one's linens is a fine old tradition, here taken to an extreme. We made a pattern by enlarging letters on a photocopier until they were almost as big as our thirty-six-inch napkin, and asked an embroiderer to do the needlework.

Coq au Champagne

This twist on classic coq au vin can be made ahead of time and reheated before serving.

TO SERVE 2

2 poussins (young chickens) or Cornish hens, quartered

6 shallots, minced

1 large carrot, peeled and finely diced

1 bouquet garni (10 crushed peppercorns, 4 sprigs fresh thyme, 2 crumbled bay leaves, and several parsley stems, all tied up in cheesecloth)

1 bottle dry champagne

6 ounces slab bacon, cubed

2 teaspoons olive oil

1 teaspoon tomato paste

2 tablespoons all-purpose flour

Salt

2 teaspoons unsalted butter

½ pound white mushrooms, stemmed and quartered

Freshly ground pepper

2 tablespoons cognac

1 cup red or white pearl onions, peeled

1 cup water

1 teaspoon sugar

2 sprigs fresh tarragon

1. In a large bowl, combine poultry with shallots, carrot, and bouquet garni. Add half the bottle of champagne. Marinate overnight.
2. Remove poultry from marinade and pat dry. Strain marinade, reserving both solids and liquid. In a large frying pan, cook bacon over medium heat until crisp. Remove and drain. Pour all but about 1 tablespoon of bacon drippings from pan.
3. Heat drippings with the oil and add poussin pieces skin side down. Cook on both sides over medium heat until well browned, about 3 minutes per side. Remove from pan and keep warm.
4. Add reserved marinade vegetables to pan and cook over low heat, stirring constantly, for 3 minutes. Add tomato paste; cook for 1 minute. Add flour; cook for 2 minutes. Add reserved marinade liquid and bouquet garni; bring to a boil. Lower heat to a simmer and season with salt. Simmer until slightly thickened, about 5 minutes.
5. Meanwhile, melt butter in a medium sauté pan over high heat and cook mushrooms until softened. Add salt and pepper to taste.
6. Add poultry pieces, mushrooms, and cognac to sauce. Cook over low heat, partially covered, until meat is tender, about 20 minutes. Add champagne as needed to keep sauce from becoming too thick.
7. Meanwhile, place pearl onions, water, and sugar in a small saucepan. Cook over low heat until most of liquid evaporates and onions are soft, 10 to 15 minutes.
8. Add bacon, onions, and tarragon to poussin and cook 5 minutes longer. Remove bouquet garni, season to taste, and serve.

Roasted Pepper Hearts with Parsnip Puree

Individual heart-shaped white porcelain molds with perforated bottoms work nicely for this pretty side dish.

TO SERVE 2

1 large sweet red pepper

4 parsnips

Salt

2 tablespoons unsalted butter

¾ cup hot milk

Freshly ground pepper

1 large egg yolk

1. Roast pepper by setting it directly over the flame of a gas burner and turning until skin is completely blackened. (If you don't have a gas stove, broil on top rack of oven.) Cool in a small paper bag.
2. Peel pepper (do not rinse). Pull out stem and seeds; discard. Cut along one indentation and lay flat. Cut along natural separations into heart-shaped sections. Line two 3¼-inch porcelain molds with pepper pieces. Cover outsides of molds with foil and set aside.
3. Peel parsnips and cut into 2-inch pieces. Put in a small saucepan and cover with water. Add a pinch of salt and bring to a boil. Lower heat and simmer until soft, about 10 minutes. Drain.
4. Heat oven to 350°. Put parsnips and butter in work bowl of a food processor. Process parsnips, slowly adding enough milk to make a puree. Add salt and pepper to taste. Mix in egg yolk. Fill molds with puree; bake until slightly puffed and golden. Carefully invert molds directly onto serving plates.

{ Vegetable hearts

Almost any root vegetable can be cut into shapes with cutters, blanched, and sautéed for a pretty and delicious dish. For this one, we used carrots and turnips. We cut the vegetables into quarter-inch-thin slices, then made cut-outs with tiny heart-shaped cutters. The hearts were dropped into boiling water for one minute, plunged into a bath of ice-cold water, then drained and set aside. Just before serving, we sautéed them in unsalted butter over medium heat until soft, about five minutes.

A NINETEENTH-CENTURY Aubusson chair, a velvet patchwork tablecloth, gold-lipped china, antique silver and crystal, and Double Delight roses set the tone for domestic romance.

Food of the gods } *For some, chocolate is divine. Others consider it to be the definition of love itself.*

Soufflé tips }

The key to a soufflé lies in the egg whites, in how stiff and voluminous they become in the beating and in how lightly they are folded into the other ingredients. Any type of beater may be used—electric, rotary, or a wire whisk—but the bowl and the beater must be clean and dry: the slightest trace of moisture or debris, including bits of egg yolk or shell, will keep the whites from inflating. Copper bowls are preferred because copper acts as a stabilizer; aluminum and plastic are not recommended.

Do not let beaten egg whites sit. They must be folded gently into the chocolate immediately upon being beaten, and just until blended—handle as little as possible.

Consistency in oven temperature is paramount with soufflés. When the soufflé is ready, open the oven door only long enough to slide it safely inside. And don't open the oven again except to check that it's done.

RICH CHOCOLATE SOUFFLÉ

This soufflé is simple to make and won't fall as easily as some do.
TO SERVE 2 TO 4

   4 ounces bittersweet chocolate, cut into small pieces
   4 tablespoons (½ stick) unsalted butter
   2 tablespoons Grand Marnier or other liqueur, or strong coffee
   3 large egg yolks and 5 large egg whites, at room temperature
      Pinch of cream of tartar
      Confectioners' sugar for dusting

1. Heat oven to 450°. Butter a 4-cup soufflé dish and coat with granulated sugar. If desired, attach a parchment-paper collar, securing it with kitchen string. Set aside.
2. Combine chocolate and butter in a small heat-proof bowl, and set over a saucepan of barely simmering water until almost melted. Remove from heat and stir until completely melted. Stir in liqueur or coffee and egg yolks.
3. Beat egg whites with cream of tartar until stiff peaks form; don't overbeat. Whisk a quarter of the egg whites into the chocolate mixture. Fold in remainder with a rubber spatula. Pour into dish.
4. Bake on bottom rack for 5 minutes. Lower temperature to 425° and continue baking, 10 minutes for a moist center, 15 minutes for a dry center. Dust with confectioners' sugar and serve.

CHOCOLATE ROMANCE

We iced this flourless "soufflé" cake, but it could just be dusted with confectioners' sugar.

TO SERVE UP TO 20

  13 ounces bittersweet chocolate
  13 ounces (26 tablespoons) unsalted butter
    Pinch of salt
   6 large egg yolks, at room temperature
   1 large whole egg, at room temperature
   1 cup sugar
  13 large egg whites, at room temperature
    Chocolate Ganache (recipe follows)

1. Heat oven to 300°. Butter one 5-by-2-inch and two 9-by-2-inch round cake pans. Line bottoms with parchment paper, butter again, and coat with sugar.
2. Combine chocolate, butter, and salt in a small bowl. Place over barely simmering water until almost completely melted. Remove from heat, and stir until smooth.
3. Beat together egg yolks, whole egg, and ⅔ cup of the sugar on high speed until pale and fluffy. Transfer to a large bowl.
4. Thoroughly wash and dry mixing bowl and beater. Beat egg whites on low speed until frothy. Turn up to high and beat until soft peaks form. Slowly add remaining sugar; beat until stiff peaks form.
5. Add chocolate and egg whites all at once to egg mixture; fold in until well combined. Divide among cake pans. Bake larger cakes 45 minutes, smaller one 35 minutes. Cool in pans, then turn out onto wire racks. Peel off parchment. Turn layers over and trim tops flat.
6. Whip half of ganache. Place one 9-inch layer, bottom side down, on a lazy Susan and cover top with about ¾ cup whipped ganache. Place other 9-inch cake, bottom side up, on frosted layer. Cover with whipped ganache, smoothing over sides and top. Frost 5-inch cake with whipped ganache. Chill cakes until firm.
7. Place both cakes on wire racks set over parchment paper. Pour warm ganache onto centers of cakes, letting it drip down sides. Scrape up excess, rewarm, and use again if necessary; use a spatula to patch any bare spots. Allow ganache to set.
8. Transfer larger cake to serving plate. Insert three wooden skewers in a small circle in center and cut to height of cake. Place smaller layer on skewers. Decorate with chocolate leaves (see page 36) and twigs dipped in chocolate.

CHOCOLATE GANACHE

Whipped ganache is best for filling; unwhipped makes a glossy frosting.

TO MAKE 4 CUPS

  1½ pounds bittersweet chocolate, chopped into small pieces
  2½ cups heavy cream

1. Put chocolate in a dry metal bowl. In a small saucepan, scald cream; pour immediately over chocolate. Let stand for a few minutes, then stir gently until smooth.
2. Pour half the ganache into a bowl and refrigerate until cold but not solid. Whip until lighter in color and stiff enough to spread; use as soon as possible. Keep remainder over a bowl of warm water until ready to use.

Choosing chocolate }

Your chocolate desserts depend entirely on the quality of chocolate used; it really is worth buying the best quality you can find. Taste and texture vary considerably among brands, depending on the blend of the beans, the type and amount of flavorings (like vanilla), and the proportion of pure chocolate liquor (cocoa solids and cocoa butter), sugar, and extra cocoa butter. Marilyn Mueller, who taught us how to make the chocolate confections on the following pages, recommends Valhrona chocolate from France or Callebaut from Belgium. Other confectioners and pastry chefs choose Swiss Lindt and U.S. Ghirardelli. Each brand has its own distinct character and its own characteristics in baking; you'll want to experiment to find the one you like best.

CHOCOLATE ROMANCE,
on an amethyst Depression-
glass stand, is an airy two-
tiered "soufflé" of a cake, filled
and frosted with velvety
ganache and crowned with
handmade chocolate
leaves (see following pages
for instructions).

Tempering }

Chocolate for making candies or decorations should be glossy, without any trace of bloom, or surface cloudiness. To keep this look after molding, it must be tempered: melted and cooled in a special process. Measure the chocolate needed and cut off a one-third chunk. Break up the remainder and melt in a dry metal bowl over a hot-water bath (water should be just below boil and off burner). When chocolate has reached 100° on a candy thermometer, remove from water bath and add remaining chunk. Stir until melted chocolate cools to 85°; remove any that's unmelted. Replace bowl over water and heat, stirring, to 90° (for bitter- or semisweet) or 85° (for milk or white). Use right away.

To make "modeling" chocolate (for bows, right), combine a pound of melted tempered chocolate with seven ounces of light corn syrup. Knead mixture until smooth and pliable by feeding pieces six or eight times through a pasta machine on the widest setting.

•confectionery

1. For chocolate BOWS, feed modeling mixture (see left) into pasta machine on thinnest setting. Make five eight-inch strips (for bow loops and knots) and four others a bit longer (for streamers). Trim sides and ends of longer strips.

2. Slide edible gold leaf from paper backing onto all strips, and press firmly to secure.

3. Cut one eight-inch strip in half for knots. Gather each end of remaining four loops.

4. Join gathered loop ends, gilded side out, and pinch together.

5. Using melted chocolate as glue, form each bow into two loops wrapped with a knot. Notch streamer ends, curl, and attach. Let bow harden overnight.

For CABBAGES, use tempered chocolate (left) which can be molded onto clean, dry savoy-cabbage or radicchio leaves (or indeed any highly modeled leaf).

6. Make about 15 leaves of graduated sizes, molded on leaf fronts and backs to vary shapes. With a synthetic bristle brush, coat leaf almost to edge, forcing chocolate into indentations.

7. With fingers, pat on more chocolate to an eighth of an inch thick. Chill for ten minutes.

8. Gently peel away leaf.

9. Using melted chocolate as glue, join the two smallest leaves along one side and bottom; chill for ten minutes. Repeat procedure with progressively larger leaves.

10. As cabbage grows, support with crumpled foil.

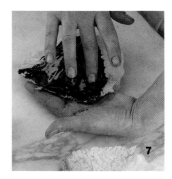

HOLLOW PEARS are formed by slightly thickening the chocolate lining of two half molds and "gluing" them together with chocolate when dry. We made leaves and stems from modeling chocolate to finish our fruits.

easter sunday

spring breakfast

buttermilk french toast
with
warm berry compote

poached eggs
on
rounds of polenta

blanched asparagus

} 3

A DELICATE VASE for
spring's blooms is made by
pricking a pea-size hole in one
end of a raw egg with a
heavy needle, a tiny one in the
other, and blowing out the
contents. Rinse and dry shell,
then seal small hole with
a glue gun.

BUTTERMILK FRENCH TOAST

If the bread is a day or two old, it will take a bit longer to absorb the egg mixture; soak as long as needed.

TO SERVE 10

- 8 large eggs
- 2 cups buttermilk
- ½ teaspoon cinnamon
- Freshly grated nutmeg
- Pinch of salt
- ½ cup sugar
- 2 loaves French bread
- Butter or vegetable oil for frying

1. Combine eggs, buttermilk, cinnamon, nutmeg, salt, and sugar, in a medium bowl. Whisk together until thoroughly combined.

2. Cut bread on an angle into ¾-inch-thick slices. Thoroughly soak in egg mixture. Chill, covered, on a baking sheet for 1 hour.

3. In a large frying pan over medium heat, heat a small amount of butter or vegetable oil. Cook slices in batches until golden brown on both sides. Keep warm in oven on lowest setting until ready to serve. Serve with butter and Warm Berry Compote (recipe follows).

WARM BERRY COMPOTE

This compote, a fresh alternative to maple syrup, is also delicious with pancakes or waffles.

TO SERVE 10

- 2 teaspoons unsalted butter
- ½ cup sugar
- 2 tablespoons fresh orange juice, strained
- ½ pint fresh blueberries, washed and picked over
- ½ pint fresh raspberries
- ½ pint fresh blackberries
- 1 pint fresh strawberries, washed, hulled, and cut in half

1. In a medium sauté pan over medium heat, melt butter. Add sugar and orange juice; cook until sugar begins to dissolve, about 2 minutes.

2. Add blueberries and cook until they begin to release juice, about 1 minute. Add raspberries, blackberries, and strawberries and cook until soft and ready to burst, about 2 minutes, depending on ripeness. Shake pan gently or use a rubber spatula to stir carefully (do not crush berries). Serve immediately.

Bloody Marys are the classic breakfast drink, and don't need the alcohol to be delicious (in that case, they're called Virgin Marys). To make Bloody Marys for ten, place thirty-two ounces tomato juice, the juice of one lemon and one lime, one teaspoon freshly ground pepper, one-half teaspoon salt, eight drops Tabasco, one tablespoon Worcestershire sauce, and two tablespoons horseradish in a large jar. Shake to mix, then refrigerate until thoroughly chilled. Trim five celery stalks and cut in half lengthwise. Cut one end of each stalk into thin strips and refrigerate in a bowl of water until ready to use. Pour one shot of vodka into each glass. Add mix, and stir to combine. Garnish with celery stalks, stripped side up; serve.

FRENCH TOAST was traditionally eaten in the south of
France on feast days. Here,
warm berry compote smothers
buttermilk French toast
served on old French rectory
china (each plate features
a monastic scene).

POACHED EGGS ON ROUNDS OF POLENTA

The milk helps give this polenta a creamy texture.
TO SERVE 10

   3 cups milk

   4 cups water

   1 teaspoon salt

  1½ cups yellow cornmeal

  1½ tablespoons unsalted butter, plus additional
     for frying

   ⅓ cup freshly grated Parmesan
     Freshly ground pepper

  10 large eggs
     Herb Beurre Blanc (recipe follows)
     Chopped chives, for garnish

1. Lightly butter a 9-by-13-inch baking dish. Set aside. In a large saucepan, combine milk, water, and salt. Bring to a boil and slowly sprinkle in cornmeal, whisking constantly to break up lumps. Cook over low heat, stirring constantly with a wooden spoon, for 15 minutes.

2. Stir in butter, cheese, and pepper to taste. Pour into prepared dish, cover with plastic wrap, and refrigerate until firm (polenta can be refrigerated for up to 2 days).

3. In a nonstick frying pan over medium heat, melt a small amount of butter. Using a 3-inch round cookie cutter or a large glass, cut out 10 circles of polenta. Cook until brown on both sides, about 3 minutes per side. Transfer to a baking sheet and keep warm in oven on lowest setting.

4. In a large saucepan, bring about 3 inches of lightly salted water to a boil, then turn down to a bare simmer. One at a time, carefully crack eggs into a small shallow bowl, then gently slide into water. Poach two or three at a time for 3 to 5 minutes. Remove with a slotted spoon and drain well. Continue until all eggs are poached.

5. On serving plates, top each polenta round with a poached egg; spoon a little Herb Beurre Blanc on top, sprinkle with chopped chives, and serve immediately.

Note: Eggs can be poached ahead of time and refrigerated in a bowl of cold water. To reheat, place in a pan of hot water for a few minutes, drain, and serve.

BLANCHED ASPARAGUS

TO SERVE 10

2 pounds asparagus

Trim woody ends from asparagus and peel the bottom two inches of stems. Blanch in lightly salted water for about 5 minutes or until desired tenderness is reached; drain. Place several spears on each plate, alongside poached eggs; top with Herb Beurre Blanc if desired.

HERB BEURRE BLANC

This sauce should be made as close to serving time as possible; if reheated, it will separate. Use the herbs in any combination.

TO MAKE ABOUT 1 CUP

3 shallots, minced

2 cups dry white wine

½ pound (2 sticks) cold unsalted butter

Salt and freshly ground pepper

2 tablespoons chopped fresh tarragon, basil, parsley, and chives

1. In a small saucepan, combine shallots and wine. Bring to a boil, reduce heat to medium, and simmer until liquid is reduced to 2 tablespoons, about 20 minutes.

2. Turn down heat to lowest possible flame. Whisk in butter 1 tablespoon at a time, adding a piece as previous one melts. Don't allow sauce to become too hot.

3. Season to taste with salt and pepper and keep over a pan of warm water. Just before serving, stir in herbs.

{Marzipan eggs

Marzipan makes a very delicious treat when formed into miniature Easter eggs. Buy the best quality marzipan or make your own (see a cookbook such as The Joy of Cooking). *Shape the paste into eggs, brush on food coloring (we like paste coloring for the variety of palette and quality of colors), and roll in granulated sugar.*

a fine spring day

salads

& growing greens

spring salad with citrus vinaigrette
caesar salad
herbed tomato salad
grilled shiitake mushrooms
on japanese greens
pencil asparagus with tarragon oil
mesclun salad
frisée with sautéed shrimp,
marinated olives, and capers

} 4

THE FIRST BITE of spring combines the near-tartness of radicchio caesar with peppery lollo biondo and perella. Borage, pansy, and yellow and orange nasturtium petals provide yet another dimension of flavor and color.

SPRING SALAD WITH CITRUS VINAIGRETTE

This is a tender, delicate salad, perfect for celebrating the first real day of spring. Any mix of attractive, soft-leafed lettuces will do; you could also use mesclun. Don't substitute different flowers, though, unless you are sure your choice is edible.

TO SERVE 6

1 tablespoon fresh grapefruit juice

½ tablespoon champagne vinegar

4 tablespoons avocado oil

Salt and freshly ground pepper

2 handfuls perella lettuce (or red oak-leaf)

2 handfuls radicchio caesar (or Belgian endive)

2 handfuls lollo biondo (or baby bibb lettuce)

6 pansies

6 nasturtiums

6 borage blossoms

Whisk together juice, vinegar, and oil; season to taste. Toss greens with this dressing, and top with flowers.

CAESAR SALAD

This Caesar salad, with cubes of French bread sautéed in garlicky olive oil, is wonderful for a quick lunch or light supper.

TO SERVE 6

6 cloves garlic, peeled

½ cup extra-virgin olive oil

½ baguette, cut into ¾-inch cubes

Salt and freshly ground pepper

3 egg yolks

1 2-ounce can anchovy fillets, drained and coarsely chopped

¾ cup freshly grated Parmesan

4 tablespoons freshly squeezed lemon juice

6 heads baby romaine lettuce, torn into pieces

1. Crush garlic with the flat side of a knife. Add to the olive oil, and let stand for at least an hour.

2. Heat 3 tablespoons of the garlic-flavored oil in a nonstick pan over low heat. Sauté bread until golden brown, about 5 minutes. Drain on paper towel, and salt and pepper to taste. Set aside.

3. Combine all ingredients, including remaining garlic oil (discard cloves), and mix well. Season to taste, and serve immediately.

EACH INGREDIENT *in a Caesar salad, from the fresh Parmesan cheese to the anchovy fillets, has a gutsy taste essential to the balance of the dish.*

ERBED TOMATO SALAD

Tomatoes and basil are a classic combination; this colorful salad dressed with basil-infused oil offers another method of marrying them. Like all infused oils, this one is easy to make and adds intense flavor.

TO SERVE 6

- 1 pint red cherry tomatoes, halved
- 1 pint yellow pear tomatoes, halved
- 1 tablespoon coarsely chopped fresh Italian flat-leaf parsley
- 1 leaf lemon basil, rolled and cut into thin strips with a knife
- 1 tablespoon fresh chervil leaves
- ⅓ cup basil oil (see note)

Salt and freshly ground pepper

In a salad bowl toss together all ingredients except salt and pepper. Season immediately before serving. Note: To make basil oil, pick the leaves from 2 large bunches of basil and gently pack into a wide-mouthed pint bottle or jar. Fill the jar almost to the top with extra-virgin olive oil and let sit, uncovered, at room temperature for 2 hours. Cover and store in refrigerator. The oil will be ready for use in 1 week; it can be kept in the refrigerator for up to 4 weeks or in the freezer for up to 4 months. Use the oil for dressings or for sautéing meat, fish, and vegetables, especially potatoes.

a salad palette } *Clockwise from top left, mushrooms marinating; grilled shiitakes on Japanese greens; pencil asparagus; mesclun.*

GRILLED SHIITAKE MUSHROOMS ON JAPANESE GREENS

Use unfamiliar greens to spark new recipes, like this mixture of watercress, pepper cress, mizuna, tat soi, and amaranth.

TO SERVE 6

  ½ cup each virgin olive oil and canola oil

  4 cloves garlic, peeled and crushed

  4 tablespoons balsamic vinegar

  8 sprigs each fresh thyme and oregano

  18 large shiitake mushroom caps

  6 generous handfuls of mixed greens

   Salt and freshly ground pepper

1. In a shallow bowl, mix together oils, garlic, and 2 tablespoons of vinegar. Crush the herbs gently between fingers to release flavor, and add to marinade. Marinate mushroom caps for 1 hour.

2. Heat a grill to medium heat. Lightly salt and pepper mushrooms, and grill them gill side down for 2 to 3 minutes, until soft and lightly marked; turn and cook for 2 to 3 minutes more.

3. Strain marinade and add remaining vinegar. Season to taste. Add mixed greens and mushrooms, toss to lightly coat, and serve.

MESCLUN SALAD

Mesclun comes from the Provençal *mesclumo* ("a mixture") and means a selection of wild and cultivated baby greens. The best will come from your own garden, but mesclun ready to eat is now sold around the country, its content changing with the seasons.

TO SERVE 6

  6 tablespoons extra-virgin olive oil

  2 tablespoons champagne vinegar

   Salt and freshly ground pepper

  6 handfuls mesclun

Whisk together oil and vinegar; season to taste. Toss greens with dressing and serve.

PENCIL ASPARAGUS WITH TARRAGON OIL

Slim, tender asparagus is one of the great treats of early spring. We served ours with Yellow Tomato Vinaigrette (recipe follows).

TO SERVE 6

  2 bunches pencil-thin asparagus (about 4 dozen spears), trimmed

  3 generous handfuls marvel lettuce

  ⅓ cup tarragon oil (see Note)

   Salt and freshly ground pepper

  6 leaves fresh opal basil, for garnish

1. Tie the asparagus loosely with kitchen string, and boil in salted water for 4 to 5 minutes, or until the spears can be bent when lifted from the water. Plunge into ice water, then drain.

2. Divide the marvel lettuce among 6 plates. Toss the asparagus gently with the tarragon oil, and season to taste; place on lettuce. Top with Yellow Tomato Vinaigrette, if desired, and garnish with opal basil.

Note: To make tarragon oil, plunge ½ cup fresh-picked tarragon leaves into boiling water for 15 seconds, drain, then plunge into ice water. Drain again; squeeze water out of leaves. Process leaves and 1 cup canola oil using a minichopper, until crushed. Let infusion stand at room temperature for 6 to 12 hours, then refrigerate in a lidded container. The oil will be ready to use after a day and can be refrigerated for up to 4 weeks or frozen for up to 4 months

YELLOW TOMATO VINAIGRETTE

This pretty golden tomato vinaigrette is an excellent accompaniment to asparagus and grilled or broiled fish or meat.

TO MAKE 1 CUP

  3 medium yellow tomatoes, cored, peeled, seeded, and diced

  4 tablespoons pure olive oil

  2 tablespoons extra-virgin olive oil

  2 tablespoons champagne vinegar

  1 teaspoon each chopped fresh tarragon, savory, and chervil

Salt and freshly ground pepper

Mix diced tomatoes, oils, vinegar, and herbs in a glass, steel, or pottery bowl. Season to taste and let sit for 1 hour.

Salad greens are packed with nutrition; maximize these benefits by carefully choosing and storing them. Look for firm, unblemished leaves; discard outer leaves of large heads. Gently rinse the whole leaves in a sinkful of cold water. Dry in a salad spinner, packing loosely so they don't bruise. Tear greens; never cut. Small leaves can be left whole. Most greens can be refrigerated for up to two days. Place clean, dry leaves in a self-sealing plastic bag with a single sheet of paper towel to absorb moisture and prevent rotting.

Do not use copper, aluminum, or iron for serving or mixing salad; the dressing's acid will react with the metal. Glass, ceramic, stainless steel, or wood are fine. If you use a wooden bowl, keep it well oiled, and clean it with a paper towel—never wash it.

f

FRISÉE WITH SAUTÉED SHRIMP, MARINATED OLIVES, AND CAPERS

With some crusty French bread and a basket of fruit, this Mediterranean-style salad would make an excellent meal. Its special quality, though, depends on finding the right olives: oil-cured are very different from canned, and it's worth the extra effort to find them. The shrimp should be a substantial size: ask for "16-20" shrimp, meaning 16 to 20 shrimp to the pound.

TO SERVE 6

  1 pound French black oil-cured olives
10 sprigs fresh rosemary
    Zest of 1 lemon, cut into strips
  2 cups extra-virgin olive oil
  1 pound green Provençal olives
  5 pink peppercorns
  5 green peppercorns
  5 white peppercorns
  3 star anise
10 sprigs fresh thyme
24 large shrimp (about 1¼ pounds), peeled and deveined
  2 heads frisée lettuce, torn into pieces
    Juice of 1 lemon
  3 tablespoons large capers, drained
    Salt and freshly ground pepper

1. In a covered glass, steel, or pottery bowl, combine the black olives, rosemary, lemon peel, and 1 cup extra-virgin olive oil. In another bowl, combine the green olives, peppercorns, star anise, thyme, and remaining 1 cup oil. Let the olives marinate from 6 hours to a week

2. Season the shrimp with salt and pepper, and sauté in 2 tablespoons olive oil from the black olives over highest heat until just done, about 3 to 4 minutes.

3. Whisk together ¼ cup oil from the black olives and the lemon juice in a large bowl. Toss frisée in this dressing; top with shrimp, some of the drained olives, and capers. Season to taste. Serve the additional olives, separately, with French bread to soak in olive-oil marinade.

MEDITERRANEAN ACCENTS—
star anise, rosemary sprigs,
capers, green Provençal and
black oil-cured French olives,
and Greek feta cheese—can
all lend their flavor to a
hearty salad.

•growing salad greens

Salad greens, among the easiest, most beautiful vegetables to grow, usually take only six weeks from sowing to harvest. For indoor plants, you can start seeds any time of year. For plants that are destined for the outdoors, you'll need a planting schedule: you don't want to start tomato plants in February that can't go outside until June.

1. Martha propagates her seeds in a small lean-to greenhouse, but a warm basement with grow lights can make a fine growing area, and even a warm spot near a sunny window will do in a pinch. 2. Use a sterile growing medium—a mix of peat, vermiculite, and sand is perfect and as conveniently available as commercial potting soil—to eliminate invasion by stray seedlings. 3. These peat pots are good for large seeds, like cabbages, okra, eggplants, and peppers. Fill with soil to within half an inch of the top, and gently press down. 4. Smaller seeds do better in these reusable plastic plugs. 5. Tiny seeds, like lettuce (these are seeds of "Biondo Lisce") and herbs should be scattered in small plastic boxes. Don't be tempted to sow too thickly: at transplanting time, you'll want to separate the seedlings without having to untangle roots. 6. Follow planting instructions on seed packets, then use the empty packet to record the date of planting. 7. Cover seeds with a layer of dampened soil twice as deep as their circumference. 8. Pat soil down gently with the back of your hand. 9. Mark each flat with the type of seed and the date. Plastic, wood, or metal markers (like these English ones) and an indelible pen are best for this.

{ Care and feeding

Use the fine-mist spray on the garden hose to gently water the flats or pots. Cover with sheets of plastic to retain moisture. When the first seeds sprout, remove the plastic, place seedlings in direct light, and begin feeding them every five days with a weak mixture of water-soluble plant food. Water every day to keep soil just moist; turn the flats to encourage uniform growth.

5

4

When growing salad greens, don't be limited to lettuce. Almost anything goes, including edible flowers and what were once considered weeds—sorrel, dandelion. In fact, "almost any weed that grows in the garden is delicious in a salad," says Anna Edey, who specializes in growing lettuces on Martha's Vineyard. "But stay away from anything with prickles." The aniselike flavor of chervil or the mustardy bite of Japanese greens can highlight any dinner. Keep in mind that the darker the leaf, the more nutritious the vegetable: arugula is loaded with potassium, calcium, and vitamin A; lettuces provide iron and vitamin C; one teaspoon of parsley fills the minimum daily requirement for vitamins A and C; borage is said to be an effective emollient.

6

{ **Planting out**

When seedlings are about 3 inches tall, plant them out into the garden. Salad greens need rich, composty topsoil; dig holes about eight inches apart. Seedlings grown in peat pots can be transplanted pot and all (soak the pot in water before placing it in the soil). Those grown in plastic pots must be gently removed, with as much soil as adheres to the roots. Place each seedling gently in its new home, and pull the soil in around the roots to support it.

7

8

9

mother's day

ladies' luncheon

& decorating cakes

consommé with herb dumplings

navarin of lamb
with
spring vegetables

mashed potatoes with sorrel
pansy layer cake
coconut cloud
raspberry ruffle

} 5

TO CROWN THE MENU at a
lunch for her mother, Martha
Stewart designed this layered
pansy cake of meringue,
angel food, whipped cream,
and blackberry preserves,
decorated with buttercream
and just-picked pansies.

Consommé with Herb Dumplings

Consommé is simply a clarified and fortified version of stock. The second cooking intensifies the flavor and renders the broth clear.

TO SERVE 6

    2 quarts cold Chicken Stock, defatted (recipe follows)

    1 cup coarsely chopped leek greens (reserved from chicken-stock recipe)

    1 cup coarsely chopped celery tops, including leaves

    ¼ cup parsley stems, coarsely chopped

    1 cup carrots, coarsely chopped

    Several sprigs fresh tarragon or ½ teaspoon dried

    1 sprig fresh thyme or a pinch of dried

    2 teaspoons salt

    ¾ teaspoon crushed peppercorns

    4 large egg whites

    4 large eggshells, crushed

    3 baby zucchini, cut into rounds, or ¼ cup finely diced large zucchini

    3 baby yellow squash, cut into rounds, or ¼ cup finely diced yellow squash

    Herb Dumplings (recipe follows)

    6 chives, cut into 1-inch lengths

1. Heat stock to lukewarm. Combine leeks, celery, parsley, carrots, tarragon, thyme, salt, peppercorns, egg whites, and eggshells and stir into stock. Turn heat to high and stir constantly until mixture comes to a boil (it will become cloudy). As soon as the mixture boils, turn down heat to very low.

2. A crust will form on top. Make a hole in crust with a ladle to allow liquid to boil through. Ladle liquid over surface of crust several times during first few minutes. Let stock simmer for 30 minutes, then turn off heat. Let stand for 10 minutes.

3. Line a sieve with damp cheesecloth or a damp, clean kitchen towel. Carefully ladle consommé through sieve, discarding solids. Adjust seasonings. Set consommé aside or let cool and refrigerate until ready to use.

4. A few minutes before serving, bring consommé to a simmer and add zucchini, squash, and Herb Dumplings. Simmer until dumplings are heated through, 3 to 4 minutes. Garnish with chives, and serve.

Consommé—a most ladylike soup—is served in gilt-edged Paris porcelain soup plates

Kristina, one of Martha's nieces, attends the lunch in honor of her grandmother.

Table settings }

Martha has been setting the table for her mother since she was three—time enough learn all the rules, and to decide that only one matters: make it pretty. Martha's tables are famous for their eclecticism, their unique mix of museum-standard antiques, Depression-era finds, and happy inspirations. For this luncheon, Heppelwhite shieldback chairs (circa 1770) surround a table laid with Depression glassware, antique soup plates, place settings from Martha's mismatched collection of pearl-handled flatware, and old damask linens. Curved pieces of nautilus shell serve as salt and pepper cellars. An old glass fruit compote holds the centerpiece of tulips and roses; camellias tucked into each napkin add a subtle and original accent.

Martha with her mother, namesake, and teacher, Martha Kostyra.

CHICKEN STOCK

Always simmer stock over lowest possible heat, and avoid stirring, to obtain the clearest results.

TO MAKE ABOUT 3 QUARTS

   1 3-pound chicken, quartered
   2 pounds chicken bones, especially necks and backs
   2 carrots, cut into large pieces
   2 stalks celery
   2 onions, 1 quartered, 1 unpeeled and cut in half
   2 leeks, white parts only (save greens for consommé)
10 peppercorns
   1 tablespoon fresh thyme leaves or 1 teaspoon dried
   2 bay leaves, crumbled
   6 parsley stems
   4 quarts water

1. Place chicken and bones in a large stockpot and cover with cold water. Bring to a boil; let simmer 5 minutes. Drain and rinse.
2. Return chicken and bones to pot; add all remaining ingredients except for unpeeled onion. Bring slowly to a boil; simmer gently.
3. After 20 minutes, remove chicken quarters, pull off meat, and return bones to pot. Reserve chicken meat for another use.
4. Cook onion without fat, cut sides down, in a heavy skillet for about 20 minutes, or until completely blackened. (The blackened onion will add color to the finished consommé.) Add onion to stock; continue simmering for 4 to 5 hours, skimming off foam.
5. Strain stock and discard solids. Let stock cool completely, then cover and refrigerate overnight. Remove and discard any fat that has risen to the top.

HERB DUMPLINGS

For the lightest texture, precook the dumplings as close to serving time as possible.

TO MAKE ENOUGH FOR 6 BOWLS OF SOUP

   2 large eggs
1½ cups all-purpose flour
 ½ cup water
 ½ teaspoon salt
 ¼ teaspoon baking powder
   1 teaspoon chopped fresh tarragon or parsley

1. Beat eggs lightly and stir in remaining ingredients.
2. Bring a pan of salted water to a simmer. Drop tiny spoonfuls of batter into water. Simmer until dumplings are tender and rise to the surface, about 4 to 5 minutes. Remove dumplings with a slotted spoon and set aside until ready to serve; reheat in consommé.

NAVARIN OF LAMB WITH SPRING VEGETABLES

The flavor of this classic French stew improves when it's refrigerated overnight.

TO SERVE 6 TO 8

2 tablespoons vegetable oil

3½ pounds boneless shoulder or leg of lamb, cut in
    1½-inch cubes

    Salt and freshly ground pepper

3 cloves garlic, finely chopped

2 medium onions, peeled and diced

3 tablespoons all-purpose flour

1 cup dry white wine

2 cups beef stock (preferably low-salt)

1 cup canned tomatoes with juice, seeded and crushed

1 tablespoon chopped fresh rosemary or 2 teaspoons dried

2 teaspoons fresh thyme leaves or 1 teaspoon dried

1 bay leaf

½ 8-ounce package pearl onions (about 24)

16 baby carrots or 4 large carrots

½ pound baby turnips or 2 large turnips

¾ cup peas

½ pound young string beans or haricots verts, stems removed
    Mashed Potatoes with Sorrel (recipe follows)
    Fresh chervil, as garnish

1. In a large flameproof casserole, heat vegetable oil over medium-high heat. Season lamb with salt and pepper and place in casserole. Brown meat well on all sides.

2. Add garlic and diced onions and cook until onions are soft, 5 to 10 minutes. Add flour and cook until it is well browned, 3 to 4 minutes.

3. Add wine and cook for 2 to 3 minutes, scraping bottom and sides of pan. Add stock, tomatoes, rosemary, thyme, and bay leaf. Bring to a boil, then reduce heat to low; cover and cook until meat is tender, about 1 to 1½ hours.

4. Remove meat; place in a large bowl and set aside. Reduce sauce over high heat until thickened, about 10 minutes. Adjust seasonings. Skim off any fat. Strain sauce over meat, discarding solids; return meat and sauce to casserole. (The navarin can be made ahead up to this point. Cover and refrigerate for up to 2 days.)

5. Bring a small saucepan of water to a boil and add pearl onions. Boil 2 minutes and drain. When cool enough to handle, peel and set aside. Peel baby carrots; trim tops to ¼ inch. Repeat with baby turnips. If using large carrots and turnips, peel and cut into 1½-inch pieces. Add onions and carrots to casserole and simmer, covered, for 5 minutes. Add turnips and peas and simmer 5 minutes more, or until vegetables are tender.

6. Blanch beans until bright green and still crisp, then drain. Serve stew over the mashed potatoes and scatter beans atop each serving. Sprinkle with chervil and serve immediately.

MASHED POTATOES WITH SORREL

The herb sorrel has an interesting, slightly tart taste that lends real depth to creamy mashed potatoes.

TO SERVE 6

1 bunch sorrel, washed, with stems removed

2½ pounds potatoes, such as Yukon Gold, Yellow Finn,
    or Idaho

½ teaspoon salt

1-3 tablespoons unsalted butter

1½ cups hot milk
    Salt and freshly ground pepper

1. Place slightly wet sorrel in a small saucepan. Cover pan and place over medium-low heat. Stir occasionally until sorrel is completely wilted, about 2 minutes. Drain, chop, and set aside.

2. Place unpeeled potatoes in a large saucepan and cover with cold water. Add salt and bring to a boil. Turn down heat, cover, and simmer until potatoes are tender but not mushy, about 20 minutes. Drain and peel.

3. Put potatoes through a ricer into a large bowl, or mash with a potato masher. Using a wooden spoon, beat in butter. Beat in milk, a little at a time, until potatoes are smooth and creamy. You may not need all the milk. Whip with a whisk until fluffy.

4. Stir in sorrel and season with salt and pepper. Serve immediately with Navarin of Lamb with Spring Vegetables or place in a heat-proof bowl covered with foil over a pan of barely simmering water until ready to serve.

Rite of spring } *Lamb and vegetables are sophisticated enough for adult taste buds, familiar enough for children's.*

$\mathcal{P}$ANSY LAYER CAKE

Bake the meringues three days ahead, the angel-food cakes two days ahead. One day ahead, make buttercream and assemble the cake. Bring to room temperature; garnish with flowers and berries.
TO SERVE 12 TO 16

- 2 pansy templates, cut from parchment or tracing paper
- 1 cardboard base, cut using template as a guide
- 1 recipe Meringues (recipe follows)
- 1 recipe Angel Food Sheet Cake (recipe follows)
- 1 recipe Vanilla Buttercream (recipe follows)
- 1 cup blackberry preserves, melted over low heat
- 1 cup heavy cream whipped with 1 teaspoon vanilla extract
- ½ pint fresh blackberries, as garnish
- Edible pansies, as garnish (see "The Guide")

1. To make templates, enlarge the shapes using a copy machine, or draw shapes freehand within a 9-inch circle. Use templates as a guide for piping the meringue and cutting out angel-food cakes. Cut a piece of corrugated cardboard from a clean box to use as a cake base. Cover with aluminum foil.
2. Follow directions for assembly and decoration.

ANGEL FOOD SHEET CAKE

TO MAKE TWO 10½-BY-15-INCH CAKES

- 1 cup sifted cake flour
- 1½ cups superfine sugar
- 1¾ cups (about 14) egg whites, at room temperature
- 1 tablespoon warm water
- ½ teaspoon salt
- 1½ teaspoons cream of tartar
- 2 teaspoons vanilla extract

1. Heat oven to 350°. Butter two 10½-by-15-inch jelly-roll pans, line with parchment; butter and flour parchment. Set aside.
2. Sift together flour and ¾ cup of the sugar three times. Set aside.
3. Using an electric mixer, beat egg whites and water until foamy. Add salt, cream of tartar, and vanilla and beat until soft peaks form. Beat in remaining sugar a tablespoon at a time, until stiff but not dry.
4. Transfer to a large bowl. In six additions, sift dry ingredients over egg-white mixture, folding in each addition quickly.
5. Divide batter between the two pans and smooth it out. Bake for about 20 minutes, or until tops are golden brown and cakes spring back when pressed. Cool completely in pans.
6. Using pansy template as a guide, cut out one small and two large cake shapes. Wrap tightly in plastic until ready to use.

Sophie and Kristina admire the pansy cake, a beautiful end to any celebration. See the next pages for more cakes.

MERINGUES

TO MAKE ONE LARGE AND ONE SMALL LAYER

    4 large egg whites

      Pinch of cream of tartar

    1 cup sugar

1. Heat oven to 200°. Using the template as a guide, draw one large and one small pansy shape with a pencil on a sheet of parchment paper. Turn paper over and place on a baking sheet.
2. Place egg whites in the bowl of an electric mixer. Swirl bowl over a pot of boiling water until warm. Beat in cream of tartar until foamy. Add 1 tablespoon of the sugar and beat until soft peaks form.
3. Set aside ⅓ cup of the sugar. Gradually sprinkle in the rest while beating on high speed until stiff, shiny peaks form, 2 minutes.
4. Quickly fold in reserved sugar. Transfer mixture to a large pastry bag with a ½-inch-wide plain tip. On parchment drawing, pipe just inside lines and fill in center. Smooth with a spatula.
5. Bake for 1½ to 2 hours, or until the meringues are dry and crisp; let cool. Store at room temperature in an airtight container.

VANILLA BUTTERCREAM

If icing becomes too soft for piping, stir over ice water to stiffen.

TO MAKE 6 CUPS

2½ cups sugar

⅔ cup water

10 large egg whites

¼ teaspoon cream of tartar

  2 pounds (8 sticks) unsalted butter, cut into small pieces

  2 teaspoons vanilla extract

    Violet, sunset-orange, and lemon-yellow paste food coloring (see "The Guide" for information)

1. In a saucepan over medium heat, bring sugar and water to a boil; boil until syrup reaches soft-ball stage, 238° on a candy thermometer.
2. Meanwhile, using an electric mixer, beat egg whites until foamy. Add cream of tartar and beat until stiff but not dry.
3. With mixer running, pour hot syrup into egg whites in a steady stream; beat until steam is no longer visible, 6 minutes. Add butter piece by piece; beat until spreadable, 6 to 8 minutes. Add vanilla.
4. When ready to decorate cake, divide 1½ cups of the buttercream among three small bowls. Tint one bowl pale purple, one dark purple, and one orange-yellow (combine sunset orange and lemon yellow). Leave remaining buttercream white for base and filling.

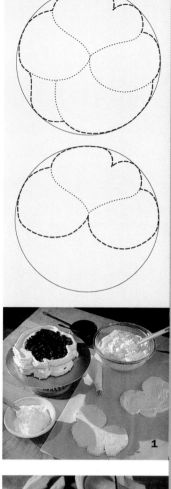

{ Cake assembly

Fit a pastry bag with a large, plain tip; fill bag with white buttercream. Place a large cake layer on cardboard base. Pipe buttercream around top edge.

Spread top of cake with blackberry preserves. Add a layer of whipped cream and a large meringue layer. Pipe buttercream around edge of meringue and spread with preserves (photo 1).

Spread whipped cream on top; cover with second large cake layer. Top with a thin layer of buttercream.

Place small meringue shape on top of cake. Pipe buttercream around edge; spread with preserves. Top with whipped cream and the small cake layer.

Spread entire cake with a thin layer of buttercream; chill until firm. Frost again, smoothing surface. Chill.

Fit clean pastry bag with a small plain tip; pipe pale-purple buttercream to outline five petals. Using a small paintbrush, feather the lines into white buttercream (photo 2).

Pipe dark-purple buttercream around outside edge of cake, then pipe three hearts meeting at center (photo 3). Feather again.

Using orange-yellow buttercream, pipe short lines radiating from center of pansy (photo 4).

COCONUT CLOUD is
decorated with freshly shaved
coconut. Pierce a coconut;
drain and discard liquid.
Crack open and remove meat
from shell. Peel off dark
brown skin. Using the blade
side of a grater, slice meat
into large flakes.

COCONUT CLOUD

The soft edges and coconut garnish give this angel-food cake an ethereal look.

TO SERVE 10 TO 12

   1 cup sifted cake flour

1½ cups superfine sugar

1¾ cups large egg whites (about 14), at room temperature

   1 tablespoon warm water

½ teaspoon salt

1½ teaspoons cream of tartar

   2 teaspoons vanilla extract

   Seven-Minute Icing (recipe follows)

2-3 cups flaked coconut (see caption, opposite)

1. Heat oven to 350°. Sift together flour and ¾ cup of the sugar four times.

2. Beat together egg whites and water until foamy. Add salt, cream of tartar, and vanilla; beat until soft peaks form, then sprinkle in remaining sugar 1 tablespoon at a time. Beat until stiff but not dry.

3. Transfer to a large bowl. In six additions, sift dry ingredients over meringue, folding in quickly but gently.

4. Pour batter into an ungreased 10-inch tube pan with removable bottom. Run a knife through batter to release air bubbles. Bake for 35 to 40 minutes, until golden brown and springy to the touch.

5. Invert immediately over the neck of a glass bottle, and let cool completely. Carefully remove sides and bottom of pan. Place on a plate, bottom side up; cover with plastic wrap until ready to use.

SEVEN-MINUTE ICING

It is best to make this icing with an electric mixer.

TO MAKE ABOUT 2½ CUPS

   3 large egg whites

1¼ cups sugar

   5 tablespoons cold water

¼ teaspoon cream of tartar

   1 teaspoon vanilla extract

1. Combine egg whites, sugar, water, and cream of tartar in a metal bowl. Set over a pot of boiling water; beat constantly for 7 minutes.

2. Remove from heat, add vanilla, and continue beating until glossy and stiff enough to spread. Use immediately.

{ Coconut cloud how-to

1. *Using thread or a serrated knife, cut a three-quarter-inch layer from top of cake. Set aside. Cut out a one-inch-wide, one-inch-deep channel halfway between center and edge of cake.*

2. *Pipe icing into channel.*

3. *Sprinkle flaked coconut over icing. Gently press on cake top, sealing in filling. Completely frost cake with remaining icing. Garnish with remaining coconut.*

RASPBERRY RUFFLE

We baked this in a heart shape, but any 8-inch pan would work.

TO SERVE 10 TO 12

  1 cup sifted cake flour
²⁄₃ cup sugar
  4 tablespoons (½ stick) unsalted butter
  1 teaspoon vanilla
  4 large eggs
    Raspberry Syrup (recipe follows)
½ cup raspberry preserves, heated
    Meringue Buttercream (recipe follows)
  1 cup heavy cream, whipped with confectioners' sugar to taste
½ pint fresh raspberries

1. Heat oven to 350°. Butter an 8-inch heart-shaped cake pan. Line bottom with parchment paper cut to fit, butter again, and lightly coat with flour. Set aside.

2. Sift together flour and ⅓ cup of the sugar twice. Set aside. Cook butter over medium heat until nut brown, add vanilla, and keep warm until added to batter.

3. Break eggs into a large bowl and add remaining sugar. Whisk over a pan of simmering water until warm to the touch. Remove from heat and whip on high speed until cool and tripled in bulk.

4. In three additions, sift flour mixture over egg mixture, folding in quickly but gently. Fold a cup of batter into hot butter, and then fold back into rest of batter. Pour into prepared pan, and bake 25 to 30 minutes. Cake will shrink away from sides of pan when done. Cool in pan 5 minutes; turn out onto a rack to cool completely.

RASPBERRY SYRUP

Génoise is always soaked with a sugar syrup to moisten cake and add flavor.

TO MAKE ½ CUP

½ cup water
  3 tablespoons sugar
  1 tablespoon framboise (raspberry-flavored liqueur)

Combine all ingredients in a small saucepan over low heat and bring to a boil. Set aside until ready to use.

MERINGUE BUTTERCREAM

If icing becomes too soft for piping, stir over ice water to stiffen.

TO MAKE 3 CUPS

1¼ cups sugar
  ⅓ cup water
  5 large egg whites
    Pinch of cream of tartar
  1 pound (4 sticks) unsalted butter, cut into small pieces
    Egg-yellow paste food coloring (see "The Guide")

1. In a small saucepan over medium heat, bring sugar and water to a boil. Continue to boil until syrup reaches soft-ball stage, 238° on a candy thermometer.

2. Meanwhile, beat egg whites on low speed until foamy. Add cream of tartar, and beat on medium high until stiff but not dry.

3. With mixer running, pour syrup into egg whites in a steady stream and beat on high speed until steam is no longer visible, about 3 minutes. Add butter bit by bit. After all the butter has been added, beat for 3 to 5 minutes, until smooth and spreadable. If the icing looks curdled at any point, don't panic: keep beating and it will smooth out. Tint as desired (see below).

1. *Cut cake into two layers. Moisten cut sides with Raspberry Syrup. Spread with warm preserves.*

2. *Using a pastry bag and a plain tip, edge with buttercream.*

3. *Fill in outline with whipped cream.*

4. *Place raspberries on one layer; top with second. Chill until firm. Frost cake thinly with buttercream, chill, and frost again. Tint rest of icing with egg-yellow paste coloring. Using a #2 round tip, pipe on zigzag lines. Edge cake, using a #7 ruffle tip.*

RASPBERRY RUFFLE,
baked in a heart-shaped pan.
Fresh raspberries are
tucked between two layers of
raspberry-syrup-soaked
génoise, which is then frosted
with a light meringue
buttercream. The stand is
yellow pressed glass.

graduation day

garden party

pearl balls
vegetable dumplings
seafood dumplings

fillet of beef balsamico
with red onion confit

roasted red pepper dip
mussels remoulade
cold sesame noodles

} 6

JAPANESE LANTERNS, from
New York City's Chinatown,
cost only $4.50 each, so you
can string up myriads (fitted
with twenty-five-watt bulbs)
to illuminate your garden
after the sun goes down.

•outdoor rooms

For big parties—graduations, weddings, anniversaries—the garden becomes another reception room.

1. Allow enough equipment to handle a constant turnover of food. Hibachis at one work station sit atop fire bricks to keep sparks from burning table linens.

2. These ten-by-ten-foot frame tents have an open-air feeling and their legs can be adjusted to uneven lawns, but have the tent company check the size and slope of your garden before ordering.

3. You'll need eight to ten different hors d'oeuvres, with two to three of each per guest.

4. Tray-served hors d'oeuvres should be bite-size neat.

5. Flowers from the garden, with reinforcements from the florist: ranunculuses, viburnums, roses, sweet peas, and poppies.

6. A combination of cold and hot hors d'oeuvres will prevent food gridlock.

7. Make sure many dishes can be made in advance to allow free time for the few that will need your last-minute attention.

8. At a cocktail party, no one sits down for very long, so five thirty-inch tables and fifteen chairs will do for fifty guests. Rental-supply china tends to be plain, so we brightened the tables with homemade linens: maize-colored tablecloths and napkins, with overcloths of matching organza.

Six weeks before: *Check garden for holes, roots, or stones that could trip guests. Plant grass seed and flowers. Plan guest list, menu, and work schedule. Research rental equipment, hire service staff, order tents.*

Three to four weeks: *Send hand-written invitations. Order food and specialty beverages (allow three to four drinks per guest for a two-hour party, plus plenty of bottled water and soft drinks). Order rental tables, chairs, plates, silver, and glasses, as well as lights, a generator, and extra extension cords.*

Two weeks: *Make tablecloths. Buy lighting, paper goods, decorations, nonperishables. Contact police department about potential parking problems.*

One week: *Prepare hors d'oeuvres that can be frozen.*

Three to four days: *Start buying perishables. Order ice or begin bagging from freezer (allow one pound per person, plus more for ice chests).*

Two to three days: *Cut grass, trim hedges. Put up tent to keep the ground underneath dry.*

One day: *Inventory rental items when delivered. Shop for last perishables. Make hors d'oeuvres, marinades, and sauces, and refrigerate. Hang lighting.*

Morning: *Thaw frozen food. Air out tents. Arrange centerpieces. Get help assembling hors d'oeuvres and arranging trays.*

Afternoon: *Have waiters and waitresses set up tables, chairs, serving tables, and bars. Just before guests arrive, turn on lights, light candles, and smile.*

BAMBOO STEAMERS *are beautiful as well as practical.*

PEARL BALLS

TO MAKE 40

  1 cup sweet Oriental rice

½ pound boneless chicken breasts

½ pound pork tenderloin, fat removed

2½ cups chopped shiitake mushrooms

  1 tablespoon dark sesame oil

½ cup chopped water chestnuts

  1 tablespoon chopped fresh ginger

½ cup chopped scallions

   Dash of sherry

  1 teaspoon sugar

  1 tablespoon soy sauce

½ teaspoon salt

½ teaspoon freshly ground pepper

1. Rinse rice under cold water, then soak for 4 hours. Drain and spread on a baking sheet lined with a dish towel.

2. Coarsely chop chicken and pork in a food processor. Set aside. In a small sauté pan over medium-high heat, cook mushrooms in sesame oil until soft, about 5 minutes. Set aside to cool.

3. Combine chicken, pork, and mushrooms with remaining ingredients, except rice, in a large bowl. Pinch off bits of the mixture and roll into 1-inch balls. Roll balls in soaked rice to coat completely. Place on a baking sheet lined with parchment or waxed paper. Chill for at least 1 hour. (You can also refrigerate for up to a day or freeze, tightly wrapped in plastic wrap, until ready to cook.)

4. Set bamboo steamer in a wok and add enough water to come to within 1 inch of the bottom of the steamer. Bring to a boil, place rice balls on the steamer rack 1 inch apart, cover, and steam for 30 minutes. Serve hot.

VEGETABLE DUMPLINGS

These are delicious with Spicy Dipping Sauce (recipe follows).

TO MAKE 30

   2 tablespoons dark sesame oil

   1 tablespoon chopped garlic

1½ cups thinly sliced leeks

1½ cups finely diced carrots

   ¾ cup chopped wood-ear or shiitake mushrooms

   2 cups shredded bok choy (a Chinese cabbage)

   ½ cup chopped garlic chives

   2 tablespoons chopped fresh ginger

   Salt and freshly ground pepper

   Dash of soy sauce

   2 egg whites

   Cornstarch for dusting baking sheet

   1 package round wonton wrappers

1. In a large, heavy sauté pan, heat sesame oil over medium heat. Add garlic and cook until lightly colored. Add leeks and carrots and cook, stirring often, until softened, 5 to 10 minutes.

2. Add mushrooms and bok choy; cook until wilted. Add garlic chives and ginger and cook for 2 to 3 minutes. Season to taste with salt, pepper, and soy sauce. Let cool and mix in 1 egg white.

3. Lightly dust a baking sheet with cornstarch. Brush edges of won-ton wrapper lightly with egg white. Place 1 tablespoon filling in center, and gather wrapper around it. Gently squeeze to form a lit-tle "waist." Set aside on baking sheet, covered, until ready to cook.

4. Set bamboo steamer in a wok and add water to within 1 inch of the bottom of steamer. Bring to a boil, place dumplings on steam-er rack, cover, and steam for 15 minutes. Serve immediately.

SPICY DIPPING SAUCE

For a different flavor, substitute two teaspoons grated fresh ginger for the chiles.

TO MAKE 1 CUP

   2 small hot red chiles, sliced

   ½ cup soy sauce

   ½ cup rice-wine vinegar

Whisk together all ingredients. Use immediately.

SEAFOOD DUMPLINGS

If you can't find lemongrass, substitute the zest of one lemon and a teaspoon of its juice.

TO MAKE 40

   ½ pound fresh lump crabmeat, picked over for shells

   1 pound small shrimp, peeled, deveined, and coarsely chopped

   2 tablespoons fresh lemongrass, finely chopped

   ½ cup chopped scallions

   3 tablespoons chopped fresh cilantro

   1 teaspoon salt

   ½ teaspoon sugar

   1 teaspoon freshly ground pepper

   1 package round wonton wrappers

Combine all ingredients except wrappers in a large bowl. To assemble and cook, follow steps 3 and 4 in Vegetable Dumplings recipe.

Ingredients can be ornaments: bundles of noodles decorate the tables.

FILLET OF BEEF BALSAMICO WITH RED ONION CONFIT

The beef is especially delicious when grilled, but it can also be seared in a pan and oven roasted.

TO MAKE ABOUT 40 PORTIONS

¼ cup balsamic vinegar

2 tablespoons lemon juice

1 cup red wine

¼ cup extra-virgin olive oil

¼ cup fresh rosemary, coarsely chopped, plus more for garnish

2 large cloves garlic, peeled and crushed

Salt

15 peppercorns, coarsely crushed

1 3- to 3½-pound fillet of beef, trimmed of fat

1-2 thin baguettes, or as needed to make 40 slices

4 tablespoons (½ stick) unsalted butter, plus more as needed

1 cup crème fraîche or sour cream

2 tablespoons horseradish

Red Onion Confit (recipe follows)

1. Whisk together vinegar, lemon juice, red wine, oil, rosemary, garlic, salt, and peppercorns in a large bowl. Add fillet, turning to coat well. Cover with plastic wrap; marinate overnight in refrigerator, turning meat several times.

2. Heat a grill until coals are hot. Grill fillet until medium rare, 145° on a meat thermometer, about 30 minutes. If roasting in oven, heat to 450°. Heat a large iron skillet over low heat until very hot (a few drops of water splashed in pan should evaporate almost immediately). Place fillet in pan and cook until brown on all sides, 5 to 10 minutes. Place skillet in oven; roast until meat is medium rare, about 20 minutes. Remove from pan; let fillet cool to room temperature.

3. Cut bread on a slight angle into ⅜-inch-thick slices; arrange on a baking sheet. Melt butter and brush each slice lightly. Toast in a 350° oven until golden brown. Set aside. Combine crème fraîche and horseradish. Set aside.

4. To assemble hors d'oeuvres, slice fillet into ¼-inch-thick slices. Spread a little horseradish sauce on toast and top with a slice of beef. Garnish with Red Onion Confit and additional rosemary.

RED ONION CONFIT

We served this warm confit as a garnish with Fillet of Beef Balsamico.

TO MAKE 1½ CUPS

4 tablespoons extra-virgin olive oil

2 large red onions, sliced ¼ inch thick

½ cup red wine

¼ cup red-wine vinegar

¼ cup water

2 teaspoons sugar

½ teaspoon salt

¼ teaspoon freshly ground pepper

1. Heat oil over low heat in a medium sauté pan. Cook the onions, stirring often, until very soft, 15 to 20 minutes.

2. Add wine, vinegar, water, and sugar, and raise heat to medium. Cook uncovered for about 15 minutes. Season with salt and pepper and serve.

ROASTED RED PEPPER DIP

This flavorful dip is wonderful served with fresh green beans, sugar snap peas, and snow peas.

TO MAKE ABOUT 2 CUPS

3 large red peppers, roasted

1 clove garlic

1 cup crème fraîche or sour cream

Salt and freshly ground pepper

¼ cup chopped fresh basil

1. Roast peppers over a gas flame or under a broiler until blackened. Place in a paper bag to cool. Peel and seed peppers, and cut into strips.

2. Puree peppers and garlic in blender until smooth. Line a sieve with cheesecloth and let puree drain into a bowl for 1 hour.

3. Combine puree with crème fraîche or sour cream. Add salt and pepper to taste. Chill. Add basil just before serving.

FINGER FOOD needs careful thought: guests must be able to pick up each piece neatly. Leaves provide an excellent means of transportation from tray to mouth; ensure that they are clean and nonpoisonous, like these fig leaves.

MUSSELS, *oysters, and clams—come in their own dish.*

M USSELS REMOULADE

Include a bowl on the serving tray for shells and used toothpicks.

TO MAKE 40 TO 50

 5 pounds mussels, in their shells
 1 bottle dry white wine
2½ cups water
 3 tablespoons fresh lemon juice
 2 shallots, sliced
20 peppercorns
 2 tablespoons salt
 1 bouquet garni (fresh tarragon and parsley tied up in cheesecloth)
 1 large red pepper
   Remoulade Sauce (recipe follows)
   Chopped flat-leaf parsley, for garnish

1. Soak mussels in cold water for 15 minutes. Scrub shells and remove "beard" by giving it a firm tug. Rinse well.

2. Combine wine, water, lemon juice, shallots, peppercorns, salt, and bouquet garni in a stockpot with a tight-fitting lid. Bring to a boil; simmer for 15 minutes.

3. Add mussels and cover. Increase heat to medium; cook, shaking occasionally, until mussels open, 5 to 7 minutes.

4. Remove mussels from broth and cool both separately. Discard any unopened shells, as well as the half shell to which mussel isn't attached. When cool, return mussels to broth, cover, and chill until ready to serve.

5. Roast pepper over gas flame or under broiler until blackened. Place in a paper bag to cool. Peel and seed pepper; cut in ½-inch-wide strips, then into diamonds.

6. Cut mussels from shells. Pour a little Remoulade Sauce in each shell; add mussel and garnish with chopped parsley and a red-pepper diamond. Pass on a tray with toothpicks.

REMOULADE SAUCE

If you are concerned about raw eggs, use store-bought mayonnaise and start at step 3.

TO MAKE ABOUT 2 CUPS

1 large egg

2 large egg yolks

½ teaspoon salt

Pinch of sugar

¼ teaspoon freshly ground pepper

¾ cup light olive oil

1-2 tablespoons fresh lemon juice

¾ cup vegetable oil

1 tablespoon capers, washed, dried, and chopped

2 teaspoons Dijon-style mustard

1 tablespoon chopped parsley

1 tablespoon chopped fresh tarragon

1 tablespoon chopped chives

1 tablespoon chopped shallots

1. Place egg, yolks, salt, sugar, and pepper in a food processor fitted with the plastic blade. Process until well blended.

2. With the machine running, add olive oil, dribbling slowly. Add 1 tablespoon lemon juice, then dribble in vegetable oil. Taste for seasonings, adding more lemon juice, salt, or pepper if needed.

3. Stir in capers, mustard, herbs, and shallots and serve immediately. (The sauce can also be made ahead and refrigerated in an airtight container for up to 2 days.)

{ The vagaries of nature

To keep your guests smiling, you'll want to anticipate what the day will bring. The Old Farmer's Almanac *is a good source for predicting sunset time, temperature, and the likelihood of precipitation. But you'll also want to play it safe by keeping sweaters and light jackets, hats, paper fans, umbrellas, and insect repellent on hand.*

COLD SESAME NOODLES

Vermicelli would make a good substitute for the soba noodles.

TO SERVE 25 AS AN APPETIZER

16 ounces soba (buckwheat) noodles

¼ cup plus 1 teaspoon dark sesame oil

½ cup soy sauce

¼ cup sugar

1 cup tahini (sesame paste)

3 tablespoons rice-wine vinegar

2 tablespoons water

Cayenne pepper

1 bunch scallions, sliced

½ cup toasted sesame seeds

1. In boiling salted water, cook noodles until tender, 5 to 10 minutes. Rinse in cold water until cool. Toss with the teaspoon of sesame oil and set aside.

2. In a small saucepan over low heat, combine soy sauce and sugar. Simmer until slightly syrupy, about 10 minutes.

3. In a medium bowl, whisk together tahini, ¼ cup sesame oil, vinegar, water, and soy-sugar mixture. Season to taste with cayenne.

4. To serve, toss noodles with dressing and some of the scallions and sesame seeds, reserving a few of each for garnish.

first day of summer

tuscan feast

& poppy bouquets

grilled mushrooms, fennel,
and peppers

grilled swiss chard packets
torta di riso
grilled shrimp in the shells
granita di caffè
baked stuffed peaches

} 7

MEYER LEMONS are bigger and
sweeter than other varieties;
connoisseurs insist they make
the best lemonade. Those
living in the right climate
can grow their own; the rest
of us must search for them at
specialty stores.

Al fresco seating }

Never mind the summer solstice, your first lunch out of doors is the true announcement that the season has begun. Though people have always eaten in the open, it was the Victorians, with their twin loves of comfort and country, who perfected lawn furniture. The Industrial Revolution made cast iron widely available (if unmoveable); cheap, light wicker was popularized by the advent of machinery that helped separate rattan into cane and reed. The twentieth century brought American innovations on European styles, including the simplicity of the Arts and Crafts movement and the use of French sprung steel. World War II brought tubular steel: inexpensive, light, resilient, and waterproof. Wooden furniture, like the thirties table, bench, and Adirondack-family chair at right, is a constant. Every era has classics that stand the test of time and prove that the best seats in the house are often in the garden.

•la dolce vita

There is much to be envied in the relaxed Italian style of living. Lunch, for example, is a meal that may start in mid-afternoon and continue until dessert coincides with sunset. Guests may meander from indoors to out, from dining room to semicovered portico to courtyard. This blurring of time and space inspired Martha's friend, decorator and furniture designer Tom Callaway, when he built his sprawling Los Angeles ranch house, every bit of which can be opened almost entirely to the outdoors. The setting, in turn, inspired Martha to give this California-Tuscan lunch, using fresh, local ingredients in an Italian tradition.

1. Inexpensive Mexican glass tumblers and Dempster hand-woven napkins are ready when guests are.

2. This handmade 1930s pitcher from California holds lemonade.

3. The hand-wrought-iron Butterfly grill.

4. Working up an appetite.

5. A seventeenth-century Spanish grate and thick adobe walls lend to the Mediterranean mood.

6. Los Angeles and Tuscany have similar climates, and thus similar vegetation.

7. Furniture maintains the harmony of Tom's vision: he refinished a 1930s picnic table in weathered green.

VEGETABLES are cut so they don't fall through the grill.

GRILLED MUSHROOMS, FENNEL, AND PEPPERS

Select very fresh and firm vegetables for grilling; don't salt while cooking or they will lose moisture.

TO SERVE 10 TO 15

2 pounds large wild mushrooms, such as portobello (or any large white mushrooms)

6 bulbs baby fennel, or 3 large bulbs

3 red peppers

3 yellow peppers

Extra-virgin olive oil

4 cloves garlic, chopped

Freshly ground pepper

Salt

Chopped tarragon, parsley, or basil

1. Remove stems from mushrooms. Cut baby fennel bulbs in half; if using large bulbs, cut into ½-inch-thick lengthwise slices. Quarter each pepper lengthwise and remove the seeds.

2. Toss vegetables with olive oil, garlic, and pepper, using just enough oil to coat them lightly.

3. Start a medium-size charcoal fire; when coals are medium hot, place grid as close to them as possible. Place mushrooms on hottest part of grill, gill side down. Turn after 3 to 5 minutes. Cook until caps fill with juice, then remove from grill and season with salt and herbs.

4. Repeat with fennel and peppers, but cook on a cooler part of grill. Avoid charring fennel before inside has softened; it should take 10 to 15 minutes to cook. Serve hot or at room temperature.

Once you've got your fire started—which should never be done with lighter fluid, as its odor and chemicals can penetrate food—it will take about thirty to forty-five minutes for charcoal to be ready, about an hour for wood. Flames should have subsided and coals burned to ashy red-hot embers before you start cooking.

Place food directly over coals, as heat radiates up, not out. Keep a spray bottle of water handy to douse flare-ups. To prevent sticking, rub the grill with vegetable oil and marinate nonfatty food for at least ten minutes. To test for doneness, slide a long fork underneath food and lift slowly. Stop if there's any resistance, and try again shortly. Use spring-loaded tongs to lift firm foods (swordfish, steak), a wide spatula for more delicate items (hamburgers, flaky fish).

GRILLED SWISS CHARD PACKETS

Swiss chard is much like spinach but with larger and sturdier leaves. It provides a neat package for the tomato and melted mozzarella inside.

TO MAKE 20

1-2 heads ruby Swiss chard
   2 large ripe tomatoes
   1 pound fresh mozzarella
     Salt and freshly ground pepper
     Extra-virgin olive oil, for drizzling and brushing

1. Remove 20 of the largest Swiss-chard leaves from the heads without tearing and set aside. Reserve remaining chard for another use.
2. Bring a large pot of lightly salted water to a boil. Have a bowl of ice water ready nearby. Plunge one or two leaves into boiling water for about 10 seconds, just until wilted. Cool in ice water; drain on paper towels. Repeat with remaining leaves.
3. Cut tomatoes into ¼ inch slices. Cut cheese into ¼ inch slices and trim to approximate size of tomato slices.
4. Start a medium-size charcoal fire; when coals are hot, place grill as close to them as possible.
5. Place a Swiss-chard leaf facedown. Cut out thickest part of stalk to about halfway up leaf. Assemble packets as below. Grill for 1 to 2 minutes on each side, until lightly charred and heated through.

Place tomato and mozzarella slices on chard leaf; sprinkle with salt, pepper, olive oil. Wrap leaf up and around filling, brush both sides with oil, and grill.

AN HERBED RISOTTO is baked
in the oven then turned out,
like a cake, and garnished
with freshly grated Parmesan
and sprigs of flat-leaf parsley.

TORTA DI RISO

This "torta," or cake, is good for a party, since it can be made ahead of time. It is essential that you use Italian short-grain rice; arborio is a widely available variety.

TO SERVE 10 TO 15

   6 tablespoons (¾ stick) unsalted butter, plus more for pan
  ½ cup bread crumbs
  10 cups chicken stock, preferably homemade
   1 onion, finely chopped
   2 cloves garlic, finely chopped
   1 cup finely chopped mixed fresh herbs, such as thyme,
     rosemary, basil, parsley, and oregano
   3 cups arborio rice
   1 cup dry white wine
  ½ cup grated Parmesan, plus more for garnish
     Salt and freshly ground pepper

1. Butter an 8-inch springform pan and coat with bread crumbs, shaking out excess. Set aside. In a large saucepan, heat stock to boiling, then lower to a simmer.

2. In a large, heavy saucepan over low heat, melt 3 tablespoons of the butter. Add onion, garlic, and about ⅔ cup of the herbs and cook until soft and transparent. Increase heat to medium and add rice. Stir well to coat all the grains.

3. Add wine and simmer, stirring constantly, until mostly evaporated. Add 1 cup of hot stock and simmer, stirring constantly, until mostly absorbed, about 3 minutes. Add remaining stock a ladleful at a time, stirring constantly. Always wait until one ladleful is nearly absorbed before adding the next. Continue until rice is creamy and firm but not hard in the center. The total cooking time should be about 15 to 20 minutes, but you must taste rice to judge doneness. Add remaining herbs about halfway through cooking time.

4. Stir in remaining 3 tablespoons butter, Parmesan, and salt and pepper to taste. Pour into prepared pan and cool completely. Refrigerate overnight.

5. Heat oven to 400°. Bake torta for about 30 minutes, or until heated through (test by inserting a knife into the center for 15 seconds and checking its temperature).

6. Unmold torta carefully onto a plate, sprinkle additional grated Parmesan over top, slice into wedges, and serve.

GRILLED SHRIMP IN THE SHELLS

Use the largest shrimp you can find—we used U-12s, which means there are fewer than 12 per pound—so that they remain moist and juicy.

TO SERVE 10 TO 15

   3 pounds shrimp
     Rosemary sprigs, slightly bruised
   6 cloves garlic, peeled and finely chopped
  ½ cup olive oil
     Juice of 2 lemons
     Salt and freshly ground pepper
   1 lemon, sliced

1. Remove legs from shrimp but do not peel. Cut several lengthwise slits along inner curve of each shrimp, and insert a few small sprigs of rosemary into each slit.

2. In a large bowl, whisk together garlic, oil, lemon juice, and salt and pepper to taste. Toss shrimp in marinade. Add more rosemary sprigs and the lemon slices. Marinate for 1 to 2 hours.

3. Start a medium-size charcoal fire; when coals are medium hot, place grid as close to them as possible. Drain shrimp and grill for about 3 minutes on each side, or until opaque. Serve immediately.

Provide a bowl where guests can discard shells after peeling their shrimp.

GRANITA DI CAFFÈ

This icy treat is the perfect way to end a leisurely summer meal.

TO SERVE 10 TO 15

2 cups plus 1 tablespoon sugar

8 cups freshly brewed espresso or coffee

1 cup heavy whipping cream

Dash of vanilla extract

1. Add 2 cups sugar to espresso or coffee while it is hot. Stir to dissolve, and let cool to room temperature.

2. Choose a metal or freezerproof glass pan that will fit easily into your freezer (a 9-by-12-by-3-inch pan works well). Pour cooled espresso into pan and place in freezer.

3. When edges begin to freeze, after about 30 minutes, stir with a fork and replace in freezer. Stir again about every half hour until large crystals begin to form and mixture is more solid than liquid; then stir more frequently, about every 15 minutes. The total freezing time will be anywhere from 2 to 6 hours. Finished granita should resemble shaved ice, with no liquid visible on the bottom.

4. Whip cream with vanilla and remaining 1 tablespoon sugar until soft peaks form. Layer granita with the cream in chilled glasses and serve immediately.

Note: Granita can be stored, covered, in the freezer overnight. If it solidifies, scrape and chop up with a metal spatula before serving.

BAKED STUFFED PEACHES

Serve the peaches as soon as possible after baking so the filling doesn't get soggy. Amaretti are available at Italian groceries and specialty-food stores.

TO SERVE 10

10 firm but ripe peaches, preferably freestone

20 amaretti (bitter-almond-flavored biscuits), crumbled

20 ounces semisweet chocolate, broken into small chunks

½ cup white wine

Sugar for sprinkling

1. Heat oven to 350°. Cut a hole in tops of peaches and scoop out pits, being careful not to tear the edges.

2. In a small bowl, combine amaretti and chocolate pieces. Stuff each peach with some of the mixture, being careful to pack down gently.

3. Place peaches a few inches apart in a baking dish. Pour wine into dish and sprinkle peaches with sugar.

4. Bake until peaches are soft, 15 to 25 minutes, depending on ripeness. Serve warm with the syrup that forms at the bottom of the pan.

A perfect peach on a yellow plate needs no garnish or decoration.

Most of the colorful ceramics on these pages come from Tom Callaway's collection of nineteenth-century Provençal pottery. With their blend of French, Italian, and Spanish influences, these vivid plates, bowls, and pitchers embody a "Mediterranean" style that appeals to their owner. Tom collects unique, old pieces, but these have become costly: a dinner plate can be $350; oil jugs are $350 to $1,200. Modern reproductions from France are more available and affordable, but Tom insists, "I only get excited by the old stuff." Those looking for a middle ground between antiques and the mass-produced copies should search in northern Spain and in Portugal, where a few local potters still use the old methods and the old hues: caramels, beiges, acidy greens, and unprimary reds. (Don't forget to check both old and new pottery for high lead levels before using for food; test kits are available at hardware stores.)

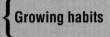
•picking poppies

Poppies make wonderful bouquets and arrangements—with one proviso. Stem ends must be seared for a second or two immediately upon picking. Use the flame from a gas stove or butane lighter: fire seals the latex sap, keeping the flowers from wilting in the vase.

1. Flanders, or corn, poppies are also given to pastel shades. **2.** Oriental poppies wake up a late-spring herbaceous border. **3.** The pink splendor of an Oriental "Cedar Hill" poppy. **4.** Poppies seem utterly appropriate as an outdoor centerpiece. **5.** Simple arrangements make the most dramatic statements. OPPOSITE: Looking into the heart of a bright scarlet Oriental poppy.

There are hundreds of species of poppies, but just four of them produce most of the flowers that deco-rate American gardens. The opium poppy (Papaver somniferum) *and corn or Flanders poppy* (P. rhoeas) *are both European annuals. The Iceland poppy* (P. nudi-caule) *is a tender peren-nial; it may not survive cold winters but, like the annuals, will self-seed vigorously, and you can help by shaking the seed pods about the plants. (It doesn't take well to trans-planting, though.) The Oriental poppy* (P. orien-tale), *is a perennial. It should generally be plant-ed late in summer, when its roots are dormant.*

The California poppy (Eschscholzia californi-ca), *funnily enough, is not a true poppy (thus it doesn't have* papaver *in its name). A tender perennial, it must be treated as an annual in cooler zones.*

Poppies tend to be forgiving in their soil demands (after all, they do well on roadsides), but they need plenty of sun to produce their vivid colors.

a wedding at home

tea party

meringue mushrooms
carpaccio teardrops
violet nosegays

asparagus with
basil tarragon dipping sauce

smoked salmon roses
cream scones

praline calla lilies
with
lemon cream

blueberry pinwheels

} 8

A KYRIA HYBRID TEA ROSE, with its tightly furled head, awaits its part in the bride's bouquet. Three or four perfect roses, stripped of their thorns (though not their leaves) and caught with a silk ribbon, will form an elegant handful.

Every small detail } *Each moment, from the first glimpse through a door to the last bite of wedding cake, is an occasion of romance.*

{ Shopping for cut flowers

Whether it's held at home or not, a wedding should be celebrated with masses of flowers. Those of us without acres of cutting gardens will rely heavily on a florist; good research ahead of time is essential.

First, consider your flowers. The bride and groom may each have favorite blooms; color will play a role; you'll need to know what is in season (though with imports from Holland and Central America so prevalent, the seasons are less and less a factor). Once you have a list of blooms, start talking to local florists about availability. While the daily stock in a small shop may be limited, any good florist will be happy to order what you want for a special occasion. If you have set your heart on garden roses, for example, he or she should be able to arrange a delivery from a wholesaler.

Should you choose to make your own flower arrangements and bouquets, your florist will have the flowers delivered in boxes. Take them out immediately, recut the stems with a sharp secateurs or scissors, and keep in a cool place in fresh water. Roses should have a day or so to open fully; all other flowers should be delivered on the eve of the wedding day.

An edible garden } *At this wedding tea, nature inspired the food: smoked-salmon roses, praline calla lilies, meringue mushrooms.*

MERINGUE MUSHROOMS

Meringue mushrooms can be made ahead of time, but because they are especially susceptible to humidity, be sure to store them in an airtight container.

TO MAKE 25

½ cup sugar

2 large egg whites

Pinch of cream of tartar

Pinch of salt

Cocoa powder, for dusting

Ganache

1 cup heavy cream

8 ounces bittersweet chocolate, chopped

1. In a heavy saucepan over low heat, bring sugar and ¼ cup water to a boil. Cover and boil on medium-high heat for 5 minutes. Remove cover and wash down any sugar crystals clinging to pan with a brush dipped in cold water. Continue to boil until syrup reaches hard-ball stage, 240° on a candy thermometer.

2. While syrup is cooking, beat egg whites in the bowl of an electric mixer on low speed until foamy. Add cream of tartar and salt and beat on medium-high speed until egg whites hold stiff peaks. With the mixer running on medium speed, add hot syrup slowly and beat for 10 minutes, or until meringue is stiff and cool.

3. Heat oven to lowest possible temperature. Spoon meringue into a pastry bag fitted with a coupler and a #1A round metal tip. To make the mushroom tops, pipe 25 quarter-size rounds onto a baking sheet lined with parchment paper. Smooth tops by dipping your finger in cold water and lightly smoothing any peaks. To make the stems, change tip to a #12 and create 25 even cylinders of meringue by pulling bag straight up and away from pan while piping. Smooth tops. Dust tops and stems lightly with cocoa powder. Bake for 2 to 2½ hours, or until meringues are dry.

4. To make ganache, scald cream in a heavy pot. Remove from heat and stir in chocolate until smooth. Let cool.

5. Spoon ganache into a pastry bag fitted with a coupler and star tip. To assemble mushrooms, pipe a small star onto bottom of each cap and attach a stem. Continue until all tops and stems are paired. Let the chocolate dry (an egg carton is ideal for this). Store in an airtight container.

CARPACCIO TEARDROPS

The meat will slice more easily if you cook it and let it cool the night before.

TO MAKE 35

½ beef eye of round (about 3 pounds)

Salt and pepper to taste

1 teaspoon olive oil

18 pound sun-dried tomatoes (about ¼ pound)

1 loaf store-bought herb or peasant bread, sliced ½-inch thick

1 cup Basil Aïoli (recipe follows)

35 whole basil leaves, washed and dried

1. Season beef well with salt and pepper and let rest for 1 hour. Heat oven to 375°. Heat oil in a large ovenproof sauté pan over high heat. Brown beef on all sides. Place in oven and roast until a meat thermometer reaches 115° (rare), 15 to 20 minutes. Let cool overnight; slice as thinly as possible.

2. Bring a pan of water to a boil. Drop in 18 sun-dried tomatoes and boil for 30 seconds. Drain and cut in half.

3. Cut bread slices into 35 teardrop shapes. Spread with Basil Aïoli. Place a tomato half on round end of bread; place a basil leaf at a 90° angle. Arrange a beef slice on top and serve.

BASIL AÏOLI

TO MAKE ABOUT 3 CUPS

1 bunch basil leaves

3 large egg yolks

½ tablespoon fresh lemon juice

1 clove garlic

½ teaspoon salt

1 cup olive oil

1. Bring a pot of water to a boil. Add basil leaves and blanch for 30 seconds. Drain; plunge into an ice bath to cool. Drain and dry.

2. Combine all ingredients except oil in a blender or food processor and puree until smooth. Slowly pour in oil and mix until combined. Store in refrigerator.

VIOLET NOSEGAYS

Edible flowers give these scalloped shortbread cookies their special look. You must be sure that the flowers you use are absolutely free from any sort of sprays. Edible flowers are available at many green-grocers and specialty-food stores across the country; see "The Guide" for mail-order sources.

TO MAKE 65

- ½ pound (2 sticks) unsalted butter
- ½ cup granulated sugar, plus more for sprinkling
- 1 tablespoon vanilla extract
- 2¼ cups all-purpose flour
- ½ cup finely chopped hazelnuts
- 2 cups cream cheese
- ½ cup confectioners' sugar
- Edible flowers, for garnish

1. Heat oven to 325°. In the large bowl of an electric mixer, cream together butter and sugar on medium-high speed until smooth. Add vanilla and flour, and mix on low speed until combined.

2. On a lightly floured surface, roll out dough to ⅛ inch. Using a 2-inch round scallop cutter, cut out scallops. With a #5 plain pastry tip, cut out a circle of small rounds around edges. Gather remaining dough into a ball and roll out again. Reuse dough only once, discarding remaining dough scraps after the second roll. Place cookies on ungreased baking sheets and bake until light brown, about 20 minutes. Let cool on wire racks, then lightly dust with granulated sugar.

3. Heat oven to 350°. Spread hazelnuts on a baking sheet and toast 10 to 15 minutes, until they give off an aroma and skins begin to blister. Shake pan occasionally. Let cool; rub nuts between your hands to remove most of the skins, then finely chop. Combine with cream cheese and confectioners' sugar. Spoon mixture into a pastry bag fitted with a coupler and a small star tip, and pipe onto cookies. Garnish with edible flowers.

Violet nosegay cookies, above; smoked-salmon roses, below.

ASPARAGUS WITH BASIL TARRAGON DIPPING SAUCE

TO SERVE 12 AS PART OF A BUFFET

- 2 pounds asparagus
- 2 large bunches basil
- 2 bunches tarragon
- 1 tablespoon olive oil
- 4 ounces crème fraîche
- 1½ teaspoons sherry-wine vinegar
  Salt
- ½ cup heavy cream

1. Bring a large pot of salted water to a boil. Trim asparagus to desired length, peeling outer skin. Boil asparagus for 30 seconds. Drain; immediately cool in an ice bath. Drain and dry.
2. Bring a saucepan of salted water to a boil. Add basil; boil for 30 seconds. Remove leaves and immediately cool in an ice bath. Repeat with tarragon. Drain leaves, squeezing out water.
3. Puree herbs and oil in a food processor. Strain through cheese-cloth, squeezing out all liquid. Discard solids. Measure 5 tablespoons liquid; fold into crème fraîche. Fold in vinegar and salt to taste.
4. In the bowl of an electric mixer, whip cream until stiff peaks form. Fold in crème-fraîche mixture. Serve immediately.

SMOKED SALMON ROSES

Have the salmon hand-sliced as thinly as possible at the deli.

TO MAKE 35

- 35 slices dense, whole-wheat bread
- 1 pound thinly sliced smoked salmon
- 1 cup Lemon Crème Fraîche (recipe follows)
  Fresh chervil leaves, as garnish

Cut bread into 35 rounds using a 1½-inch biscuit cutter. Toast until golden on both sides. Roll up salmon slices and fan out to resemble rose petals. Place a dollop of Lemon Crème Fraîche on each toast round; top with a rosette. Garnish with a chervil leaf; serve.

LEMON CRÈME FRAÎCHE

TO MAKE ABOUT 1 CUP

- 1 cup crème fraîche
- 1 tablespoon lemon zest
  Salt and freshly ground pepper
- 1 teaspoon fresh lemon juice

Combine all ingredients in a small bowl. Serve as directed with Smoked Salmon Roses.

CREAM SCONES

Scones are the quintessential accompaniment to tea.

TO MAKE 35 TO 40

- ½ cup yellow cornmeal
- 3 cups all-purpose flour
- 3 teaspoons baking powder
- ½ cup sugar
- 6 tablespoons (¾ stick) unsalted butter, softened
- 3 large eggs, beaten
- ¾ cup heavy cream
- ¾ cup currants or golden raisins
- 1 large egg yolk mixed with 1 tablespoon sugar and 1 tablespoon water, for glaze
- 6 ounces (1 bottle) Devonshire cream (available at specialty-food shops)
- 1 cup fruit preserves of your choice

1. Heat oven to 325°. Combine dry ingredients in the bowl of an electric mixer. Cut in butter to resemble coarse meal. Beat in eggs and cream until combined; do not overmix. Mix in currants by hand.
2. On a lightly floured surface, roll out dough to ½ inch. Cut into leaf shapes with a sharp knife; or cut out scones using a 2-inch scalloped or heart-shaped cutter. Place on ungreased baking sheets. Brush tops with egg-yolk glaze; bake until golden, about 25 minutes. Cool on wire racks; serve with Devonshire cream and preserves.

PRALINE CALLA LILIES WITH LEMON CREAM

The cookies are best assembled right before serving.

TO MAKE 30

- 4 tablespoons unsalted butter
- ¼ cup light brown sugar
- ¼ cup light corn syrup
- 1 teaspoon vanilla extract
- ½ teaspoon almond extract
- ¼ cup sliced almonds, coarsely chopped
- 3 tablespoons all-purpose flour
- 2 cups mascarpone (Italian cream cheese)
- Zest of 1 lemon, finely chopped
- 2 tablespoons confectioners' sugar

1. In a small saucepan over medium-high heat, combine butter, brown sugar, and corn syrup and bring to a boil. Remove from heat and stir to dissolve sugar. Add extracts and almonds. Stir in flour and let batter cool before using.

2. Heat oven to 350°. Oil a baking sheet. Using 2 teaspoons, drop ½ teaspoon of batter onto sheet, leaving at least 3 inches between cookies. Cookies will spread; don't put more than 4 on a sheet at a time. Bake for 10 minutes, or until golden brown. Let cool on baking sheet for 1 minute, then remove from baking sheet with a spatula, being careful not to tear cookie. Quickly roll one end to form a cone shape. Cool completely on wire racks.

3. Just before serving, combine mascarpone, lemon zest, and confectioners' sugar. Spoon into a pastry bag fitted with a coupler and star tip and pipe mixture into the center of each cookie.

Note: You won't need to reoil baking sheet between batches.

BLUEBERRY PINWHEELS

Shortbread dough is cut into pinwheels for an elegant look.

TO MAKE 30

- ½ pound (2 sticks) unsalted butter
- ½ cup sugar, plus more for sprinkling
- 1 tablespoon vanilla extract
- 1 large egg
- 2½ cups all-purpose flour
- 1 large egg yolk mixed with 1 tablespoon water, for glaze
- 1 cup good-quality apricot preserves
- Fresh blueberries, for garnish

1. Heat oven to 325°. In the large bowl of an electric mixer, cream together butter and sugar on medium-high speed until smooth. Add vanilla and egg; mix on low speed until smooth. Stir in flour.

2. Roll out dough on a lightly floured surface to ⅛ inch and cut out 3-inch rounds. Score each round with a knife from edge almost to center 5 times, leaving ½-inch of center intact. Carefully fold down left corner of each wedge into center and press down gently, creating a pinwheel. Brush with egg glaze and sprinkle with sugar. Bake until light brown, 20 minutes. Let cool on wire racks, then spoon preserves into center and garnish with a blueberry.

Rolled praline cookies and sugary pinwheels make a dessert bouquet.

{ The perfect day

Until the middle of this century, all brides save royalty were married at home. The women of the family made the wedding feast, the bride wore her best dress or suit, and the reception was held in the parlor—with just as many guests as the room could hold. With catered weddings costing at least $35 per head (plus rental of the location), we know many brides returning to an old tradition, holding their marriage celebration in the home of a parent or a good friend, and choosing to serve an exquisite, perfect meal—an elegant dinner, a garden lunch, or a pretty afternoon tea.

If you prefer to give a wedding at home, remember that this is the most important day in someone's life, and prepare for it accordingly. With guest list in hand, take inventory of your china, flatware, glasses, linens, tables, and chairs. Arrange for reinforcements from party-rental suppliers; ask for a sample table and chairs ahead of time so you can check the size of linens, the placement of settings. Order more flowers than you think you might need; make sure you have enough vases. Give yourself time to prepare and arrange the food; most of all, make sure you have plenty of help so you can enjoy the day.

fourth of july

a classic picnic

spicy fried chicken

stars and stripes
salad

peanut coleslaw

old-fashioned
blueberry pie

} 9

CORN ON THE COB is prepared
for grilling by pulling back
husks and removing the silk,
then tying tops back together
with string. Soaking it in
cold water prevents burning.

•picnic packing

Safely transporting food from your house to that blanket at your favorite picnic spot does not have to involve logistic gymnastics. Start by designing a menu of picnic-appropriate foods—those that keep well and are easy to eat. Then pack them in air-tight containers. A picnic hamper will accommodate all the essentials, including a frozen bottle of lemonade (which should be ready to drink by lunchtime!) to help keep the food cool.

1. Antique tin boxes lined with wax paper pack a bounty of fried chicken. Inexpensive metal clamp-edge food tins (available in New York City's Chinatown) are a good choice for juicy salads.

2. Two American classics: blueberry pie is served on enamelware plates.

3. Sparklers don't take up much room in the basket.

4. Bring a whole watermelon and a big knife (and make sure there's a lake or ocean nearby for the kids' cleanup).

5. On this holiday there's plenty of food for thought—or maybe they're just thinking about food.

6. Men's shirting fabric in a patriotic hue makes hardworking napkins.

7. Old-fashioned glass jars are great for pickling cucumbers or making iced tea (wrap loose tea in cheesecloth, tie with string, add cold water, and brew for at least four hours).

CUMBERLAND ISLAND, a
National Seashore preserve
off the coast of Georgia, is
accessible only by boat (from
Fernandina, Florida).

MARTHA'S *own fried chicken*.

SPICY FRIED CHICKEN

Soaking the chicken in seasoned buttermilk makes the meat tender, sweet, and juicy.

TO SERVE 12

For the soaking mixture:

- 1 quart buttermilk
- ½ teaspoon cayenne pepper
- ½ teaspoon salt
- 1 teaspoon freshly ground pepper
- 4 cloves garlic, slightly crushed
- 2 3-pound fryers, cut into 8 pieces each

For the flour mixture:

- 3 cups unbleached all-purpose flour
- 2 teaspoons salt
- 2 teaspoons freshly ground pepper
- 2 teaspoons cayenne pepper
- 1 teaspoon paprika
  Vegetable oil, for frying

1. In a large bowl, combine the first 5 ingredients. Add chicken pieces, turning to coat well. Cover bowl and refrigerate overnight, turning chicken once or twice.

2. Drain chicken in a colander, discarding buttermilk mixture. In a shallow pan, combine flour with remaining salt and spices. Dredge chicken pieces in flour mixture. Shake off excess; set aside on a baking sheet for about 30 minutes.

3. In a large, heavy frying pan with straight sides, heat a half inch of oil to 360°. Just before frying, dredge chicken in flour mixture again. Add to oil one piece at a time to maintain a steady temperature. Don't crowd pieces.

4. While chicken is frying, maintain a temperature of 320°. Cook for 10 to 15 minutes per side, turning once, until chicken reaches an internal temperature of 160° and juices run clear. Remove from oil with a slotted spoon; drain. Repeat until all chicken is cooked. Serve hot or cold.

On this most American of holidays it seems fitting to use those most American of dining utensils—enamelware plates and Bakelite flatware. Enamelware was humble stuff during its heyday—the 1870s through the 1930s—and popular for being lighter and tougher than china. But much was lost to the scrap-metal drives of World War II; original pieces are hard to find, and command heady prices. In the 1960s, the old shapes and patterns—like these blue-rimmed white classics—began to be remanufactured; they are still produced today.

Bakelite, "plastic with a pedigree," was invented in 1907. Collectors prize the flatware's luminous colors, which mellow over the decades, but its price is also attractive. Unlike Bakelite jewelry, it's still a bargain: four knives and forks (a knife and a fork were known as a luncheon set) in a common color (red) can be had for as little as $100.

STARS AND STRIPES SALAD

Jicama is a tuber that is similar in texture to a potato and in flavor to an apple. They are best when smooth and firm, with thin skins.

TO SERVE 12

   3 ripe tomatoes, seeded and diced

   ¼ cup sherry vinegar

   ¾ cup olive oil

     Salt and freshly ground pepper

   1 medium jicama

   1 seedless cucumber (long hothouse variety)

   1 large head red-leaf lettuce, torn into pieces

   3 heads Bibb lettuce, torn into pieces

1. Combine tomatoes, vinegar, oil, and salt and pepper to taste in a glass jar. Shake well; refrigerate overnight.
2. Peel jicama by cutting a thin slice off the top and bottom and peeling all sides with a sharp knife. Cut into slices about ⅜ inch thick. Using assorted star-shaped cookie cutters, cut jicama slices into stars. Cover with a damp paper towel until ready to use.
3. Wash cucumber well; do not peel. Cut off tips and, using a vegetable peeler, cut into long, thin strips.
4. Place lettuces in a large bowl or on a platter. Arrange cucumber "stripes" and jicama "stars" on top of lettuce.
5. Using a fork, mash a little diced tomato in the dressing. Shake well, adjust seasonings, and pour over salad.

PEANUT COLESLAW

For a mellower flavor, make the dressing a day ahead. The peanuts add a crunch to this classic summer dish.

TO SERVE 12 TO 15

- ¾ cup plain yogurt
- ¾ cup good store-bought mayonnaise
- 1 tablespoon dark sesame oil
- ¼ cup apple-cider vinegar
- ½ red onion, peeled and coarsely chopped
- 1 teaspoon celery seed
- ½ teaspoon cayenne pepper
- ½ teaspoon freshly ground pepper
- 1 teaspoon salt
- 1 tablespoon sugar
- 1 head savoy cabbage
- ½ head green cabbage
- ½ head red cabbage
- 6 large carrots
- 2 tablespoons unsalted butter
- 1 cup shelled peanuts

1. In a blender or food processor, combine yogurt, mayonnaise, sesame oil, vinegar, and onion. Puree until smooth. Add celery seed, peppers, salt, and sugar, and blend for a few seconds to combine.

2. Remove large outer leaves from cabbages and save to line the serving bowl. Shred cabbages with a large knife and set aside. Peel and grate carrots, or julienne them on a mandoline. Set aside.

3. Melt butter in a small sauté pan and add peanuts. Toast, shaking pan frequently, until brown. Do not burn. Remove peanuts from pan and let cool.

4. In a large bowl, combine shredded cabbages and grated carrots. Add dressing and mix well. Crush browned peanuts slightly with the side of a knife and, just before serving, combine three quarters of them with the cabbages and carrots.

5. Line a large serving bowl with the reserved cabbage leaves and fill with coleslaw. Garnish with remaining peanuts, and serve immediately.

OLD-FASHIONED BLUEBERRY PIE

Let the pies cool before serving, so the juices thicken a bit.

TO MAKE 2 PIES

- 1 recipe Pâte Brisée (see recipe, right)
- 6 pints fresh blueberries
- 2 cups plus 2 tablespoons sugar
- ½ cup all-purpose flour
  Grated zest and juice of 1 lemon
- 1 large egg beaten with 1 teaspoon water, for glaze

1. Line two 9-inch pie tins with dough and chill thoroughly. Roll out 2 circles of dough at least 10 inches in diameter and chill on a cookie sheet.

2. In a large bowl, combine berries, 2 cups sugar, flour, and lemon zest and juice.

3. Fill chilled shells with berry mixture. Lay pastry circles on a lightly floured board and cut a star out of each center.

4. Brush edges of bottom shell lightly with glaze and top with pastry circle, centering the star. Trim overhanging pastry to within ¾ inch and crimp edges together to seal. Chill pies for 30 minutes.

5. Heat oven to 400°. Brush pies with remaining egg glaze and sprinkle with remaining sugar. Bake 50 to 60 minutes, or until juices are bubbling and crust is golden brown.

Blue-rimmed enamelware is traditional—and practical—for picnics.

Pâte brisée }

TO MAKE ENOUGH FOR 2
DOUBLE-CRUST PIES

   5 cups unbleached all-
     purpose flour
   2 teaspoons salt
   2 teaspoons sugar
   1 cup vegetable short-
     ening, chilled and
     cut into pieces
   ½ pound (2 sticks)
     unsalted butter,
     chilled and cut into
     pieces
   ¾-1 cup ice water

1. In the work bowl of a
food processor, combine
flour, salt, and sugar.
Add shortening and but-
ter and pulse until mix-
ture resembles coarse
meal. With machine
running, slowly add
water. As soon as pastry
holds together when
squeezed, stop adding
liquid.

2. Divide dough in half,
shape into flat rounds,
and wrap in plastic.
Chill at least 1 hour or
overnight.

midsummer

supper on the beach
& outdoor lighting

white gazpacho with grapes

paella

grill roasted vegetables
with aïoli

flan

white sangria

} 10

ROWS OF CANDLE LANTERNS,
made of epoxy-finished
steel and glass, show the
way to an evening party.
Citronella scented,
they ward off bugs;
long-lasting, they will
stay lit until the last
guest is safely home.

WHITE GAZPACHO WITH GRAPES

White gazpacho has a smooth, sophisticated taste.

TO MAKE ABOUT 3 QUARTS

- 1 5-inch section of French bread
- 1 cup peeled almonds
- 4 cloves garlic, peeled
- 1 cup extra-virgin olive oil
- 2 tablespoons freshly squeezed lemon juice
- ¼ cup white-wine vinegar
- 1 teaspoon salt
  Pinch of white pepper
- 1 quart water
- 1 small bunch green seedless grapes

1. Soak the bread in ice water for 10 minutes. Remove the crust with your fingers and discard; squeeze the water out of the bread.
2. Place bread, almonds, and garlic in a blender or food processor and puree. With machine on, add oil in a trickle, to form an emulsion. Add the lemon juice, vinegar, salt, and pepper.
3. Transfer to a serving bowl, and whisk in water until gazpacho has the consistency of heavy cream. Add half the grapes and chill for 1 hour before serving. Cut remaining grapes in half for garnish.

WHITE SANGRIA

TO MAKE 1 GALLON

- ½ cup orange-flavored liqueur
- ½ cup cognac
- ¼ cup sugar
- 4 oranges, thinly sliced
- 2 mangoes, peeled and thinly sliced
- 4 bottles dry white wine, such as white Rioja
- 1 quart ginger ale

Combine first 5 ingredients in a pitcher; let sit for at least 1 hour. Pour into a large bowl; add wine. Add ginger ale just before serving.

WHITE GAZPACHO is
served on traditional glazed
Talavera ware from Spain.
The boxwood-handled knives
and forks are from France;
shells salvaged from the
beach hold coarsely ground
black pepper and sea salt.

*The summer table in a Spanish
household is likely to bear a pitcher of
sangria: wine, sparkling water, and
fruit mixed according to each family's
recipe. White sangria is an American
adaptation. We based ours on white
Rioja and ginger ale; spiked with two
liqueurs, it is more potent than its
lemonade-like looks would suggest.*

PAELLA

The best saffron comes from Spain. Though expensive, it's what gives paella its distinctive flavor. This recipe can be easily halved, but don't change the cooking times.

TO SERVE 12 TO 18

2 whole chickens, each cut into 10 serving pieces

1⅓ cups extra-virgin olive oil

3 tablespoons paprika

3 tablespoons kosher salt

2 pounds boneless pork loin, cut into 1-inch cubes
   Salt and freshly ground pepper

4 green peppers, seeded and cut into ¼-inch strips

4 red peppers, seeded and cut into ¼-inch strips

½ pound string beans, ends snapped off

6 pounds squid, cleaned and cut into 1-inch rings and
   tentacle sections

1 cup diced white onion

1 cup finely minced garlic

4 lobsters, cut into serving pieces (see Note)

1 dozen prawns (optional)

3 pounds shrimp

2 cups fresh garden peas

2 cups peeled, seeded, and coarsely chopped tomatoes

2 dozen littleneck clams

2 dozen mussels, scrubbed and debearded

15 cups chicken broth, preferably homemade, plus water as needed

8 cups long-grain rice

1 cup brandy

1 tablespoon Spanish saffron threads

2 cups frozen lima beans

2 tablespoons fresh lemon juice

1. Rub chicken with ⅓ cup of the oil, the paprika, and 1 tablespoon kosher salt; let sit for 2 hours. Heat remaining oil in a large paella pan over a gas grill set on high heat, a stove burner covered with a flame tamer, or a hardwood fire (place grid 30 inches from fire). Cook chicken in the oil, turning occasionally, until browned, about 5 minutes. Add pork, sprinkle with salt and pepper, and cook until browned, 8 to 10 minutes, stirring occasionally.

2. Add the peppers and cook for 2 minutes. Add the string beans and cook for 2 more minutes, stirring. Add the squid and cook until it loses its raw look. Add the onion and garlic; sauté for 3 minutes more.

3. Add the shellfish and sauté for 3 or 4 minutes; add the peas, tomatoes, clams, mussels, and 2 cups of the broth. Cook for 2 minutes. Sprinkle rice evenly over the whole pan, and stir until coated with oil. Add 12 cups broth and ½ cup of the brandy. With a mortar and pestle or spice grinder, combine the saffron with remaining 2 tablespoons kosher salt, then place in a small bowl and combine with the remaining 1 cup stock and ½ cup brandy. Pour over rice. Add the lima beans, adjust seasonings, and mix thoroughly.

4. Heat paella until tiny bubbles appear over the surface. (The rice should be completely covered with liquid; if it isn't, add water.) Then cook without stirring for 15 minutes, or until rice is done. (The rice that sticks to the bottom of the pan is called the *socarrat* and is the most prized part of the dish.) Sprinkle the lemon juice over the paella and let cool for 5 to 10 minutes before serving.

Note: To cut up a lobster, plunge it into a pot of boiling water for 45 seconds to kill it. Cut off the claws and crack open on one side. Remove the "knuckles" between the claws and the body and crack them on one side as well. Split tail lengthwise or cut inch-thick medallions through shell.

Paella is best made in a special shallow iron pan over a grill or open fire.

gRILL ROASTED VEGETABLES

Many vegetables have a natural protective skin that enables you to blacken the outside while perfectly roasting the inside. Cook same-size vegetables together so they will all be ready at the same time. Aïoli (recipe follows) or an herb vinaigrette is a flavorful accompaniment.

TO SERVE 8

    4 medium eggplants
    8 small leeks
    4 medium zucchini
    8 red bell peppers
    16 shallots, unpeeled

1. Remove eggplant stems and tear in half lengthwise with your hands. Trim root hairs from each leek, leaving "foot" to hold it together; trim off outer leaves, and make a lengthwise cut in leek starting 1 inch above foot. Wash thoroughly under running water to get rid of any grit. Remove zucchini stems; cut in half lengthwise.
2. Put vegetables on a grid over an open fire, skin side down if split. Turn to brown all sides, about 10 minutes total—remove vegetables when they feel soft. Let cool for 15 minutes, then remove any blackened skin, flesh, or husks. Serve with Aïoli.

AÏOLI

Aïoli is a garlic mayonnaise used as a basic seasoning all along the Mediterranean coast, from Málaga to Genoa. It is traditionally used as a dip, but it also goes well with lamb or chicken.

TO MAKE ABOUT 2 CUPS

    1 egg
    4 cloves garlic, peeled
    1 teaspoon freshly squeezed lemon juice
    2 teaspoons white-wine vinegar
    1 cup extra-virgin olive oil
      Salt and white pepper to taste

Put the first 4 ingredients in a blender or food processor, and process on high speed for 10 seconds. With the machine on, add the oil drop by drop until it emulsifies, and then in a trickle to finish. Season to taste.

fLAN

The classic utensil for melting the sugar on top of a flan is a salamander, which is first heated in coals or on a burner.

TO MAKE 6 TO 8

    2 tablespoons cornstarch
    3½ cups milk
    ⅔ cup granulated sugar
    6 large egg yolks
      Zest of 1 lemon
    1 small cinnamon stick
    ¼ cup superfine sugar

1. Dissolve cornstarch in ½ cup of the milk. Beat together granulated sugar and egg yolks until thick; beat in cornstarch mixture.
2. In a saucepan over low heat, combine remaining 3 cups of milk, the lemon zest, and cinnamon stick. Heat to boiling. Whisk in egg-cornstarch mixture; lower heat and stir until thickened. Strain, then pour into small ramekins to ⅝ inch. Let cool.
3. Sprinkle flans with superfine sugar. With a hot salamander, under the broiler, or using a propane blowtorch, heat until golden brown.

Grilled vegetables are drizzled with aïoli or with an herb vinaigrette.

Our flan's caramelized sugar top is made with a salamander.

Spanish cuisine cannot be described as casual: the Spanish take food very seriously indeed. But the concentration is on ingredients, which must be the freshest, the best, rather than on tedious preparations. As a result, many dishes are essentially picnic foods. As New York food consultant Pilar Turner (who developed the recipes on these pages) showed us, a Spanish family will make paella on the beach or in the back garden in just the way Americans will grill a batch of hamburgers.

Paella is Spain's national dish, with variations for every region, indeed for every family. It originated in Valencia, a fertile region on the southeast coast where citrus trees, rice, and olives flourish. Valencian paellas are characterized by fresh fish and crustaceans; farther inland, the dish includes sausage, poultry, and other local meats. In every region, though, paella is scented with saffron, dried crocus stamens imported to Spain by invading Moors in the eighth century. (Good saffron, by the way, should be dark orange all over, without white streaks. Purchase it from a reliable supplier; even in Spain, saffron is sometimes falsified with safflower—bastard saffron—which is redder in color.)

Flan is the national, now international, Spanish dessert. Like paella, it has regional variations, with flavorings of orange, lemon, apple, chocolate, or coconut, depending on the local produce. Everywhere it is rich with egg yolks. Food writer Penelope Casas (author of The Foods and Wines of Spain) believes that flans were developed to make use of the yolks left after egg whites were used to clarify Spanish wines. Her explanation illustrates another fine Spanish characteristic: pragmatism.

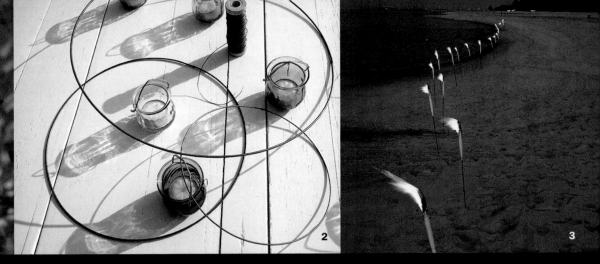

•outdoor lights

Night lighting need not be bright, but it should allow guests to see what they're eating, and allow you to serve without misstep. Plan on two sources of illumination: ambient light and table light. If your site is near a source of power, ambient light can be created with the flick of a switch. In a more remote setting, use bamboo torches, Mexican-style luminarias (votive candles bedded in sand and placed inside open paper bags), or strands of battery-operated Christmas tree lights (get the long-lasting, heavy-duty variety). For table lights, candles are best. Place tapers inside hurricane shades, or put votive candles in high-sided holders.

1. A Mexican punched-tin star holds a three-inch candle, creating a starlike glow.

2. A votive chandelier can be constructed from steel florists' rings and votive-candle holders outfitted with wire handles and hooks for hanging.

3. Citronella scent may interfere with food, so keep these torches away from the table.

4. Strands of twinkling lights twisted into the canopy will withstand gusts of wind.

5. Votive candles in glass holders perch on tree branches around the chandelier.

6. As the sun goes down, several kinds of light ensure that paths to and from the table and outdoor cooking area are visible.

7. Beachcomber torches will create ambient light for hours.

THIS GAUZY PAVILION was made by draping a store-bought tubular-steel tent frame with yards and yards of natural-colored cotton scrim. Then we wound the frame with tiny white Christmas-tree lights.

labor day weekend

tastes of provence

deviled crayfish
pistou soup
country leg of lamb
apple tart

} 11

THE SUNFLOWER was
immortalized as the symbol
of Provence by Vincent
van Gogh, who studied and
painted them after
settling in Arles in 1888.
To us it is a symbol of
summer's end, a last flash of
sunshine before the fall.

LIVE CRAYFISH await their fate in a cabbage-leaf nest.

DEVILED CRAYFISH

Crayfish can be bought live in season at a good fish market. Keep them in a plastic bag with holes punched in it until ready to use.

TO SERVE 8

   2 tablespoons unsalted butter

   1 cup finely diced carrots

   1 cup finely diced red onion

   1 cup finely diced shallots

  ¼ cup chopped parsley stems

   2 sprigs fresh thyme

   2 bay leaves

   2 pounds crayfish

   4 medium tomatoes, peeled, seeded, and diced

     Salt and cayenne pepper

  ¼ cup brandy

 1¼ cups white wine

1. Melt butter in a large sauté pan over low heat. Add carrots, onion, shallots, parsley stems, thyme, and bay leaves, and cook until very soft but not brown, about 15 minutes.

2. Turn up heat and add crayfish and tomatoes. Season with salt and cayenne pepper to taste. Cook, stirring often, until crayfish turn bright red, about 10 minutes. Add brandy and flame it; then add white wine. Cook over high heat to reduce slightly, about 2 to 3 minutes.

3. Remove pan from heat. Transfer crayfish to a warm serving platter. Pass sauce through a food mill (or puree in a food processor), then return to pan to reheat. Pour over crayfish and serve.

Ingredients of Provence }

In Provence, the olive harvest begins in November, when unripe green fruit is picked and cured in brine to temper its natural bitterness. Olives left to ripen on the tree turn black and are harvested about a month later. Those to be pressed for oil wait until January.

It takes about eleven pounds of olives to make one quart of oil. The first pressing, called "virgin" or "cold-pressed," is the best; later pressings of the pulp are aided by heat or by chemicals. (Lesser oils are fine for marinating and sautéing; choose virgin for salads. Buy by the label, not the color: greener isn't always better. Spanish and Italian oils are often green because the olives are harvested unripe; the best Provençal first pressings are pure gold.)

The unmistakable tang of the olive marks many classic Provençal dishes, none more so than tapenade, a vigorous spread made by crushing pitted black olives, capers, lemon juice, anchovies, and olive oil in a mortar. Some tapenade recipes include a few garlic cloves, garlic being the other staple of Provence. One of our favorite vegetable dishes is made by stewing fava beans with red and green peppers, fresh herbs, and a whole, unpeeled head of garlic.

A HEAD OF GARLIC,
left whole, unpeeled, and
cooked long, develops a rich,
gentle, almost buttery taste,
quite at odds with the sharp
scent of a crushed clove.

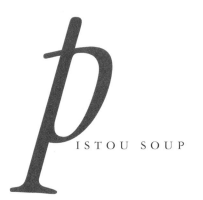

PISTOU SOUP

The depth of flavor in this soup comes from the pistou (the French cousin of pesto) and fresh vegetables, not from long cooking or previously prepared stock. It is not only typically Provençal but also fast and easy to make.

TO SERVE 8 TO 10

1 cup dried Great Northern or cannellini beans (see Note)
1 onion, quartered
1 bay leaf
½ cup olive oil
2 cups diced onion
1 cup sliced leeks
4 cloves garlic, chopped
1 tablespoon saffron, pounded using mortar and pestle (optional)
1 pound tomatoes, peeled, seeded, and diced
4 cups water
1 cup diced carrots
1 cup diced green beans
1 cup diced fennel
1 cup diced zucchini
1 cup diced white boiling potatoes
1 cup uncooked pasta (use ditalini or another very small shape)
   Salt and freshly ground pepper
   Pistou
6 cloves garlic
1 bunch basil, stems removed
3 tablespoons tomato paste
¼ cup olive oil
½ cup grated Parmesan
   Salt

1. Soak beans overnight in plenty of water. Drain, cover with fresh water, and cook in a medium saucepan with the quartered onion and bay leaf until tender, about 45 minutes. Drain, reserving the liquid.
2. Heat the oil in a medium stockpot over a low flame. Add the diced onion, leeks, and garlic, and cook until soft, about 10 minutes.
3. Add saffron, if desired; add tomatoes and water. Bring to a boil and add vegetables in the order listed, waiting 5 minutes between additions.

4. Add cooked beans and their liquid. Add more water, if needed, to cover vegetables by 1 inch, and cook 10 to 20 minutes. Add pasta and turn off heat. Season with salt and pepper, and let sit for 10 minutes.
5. Meanwhile, make the pistou. Combine garlic, basil, and tomato paste in a food processor. Pulse until coarsely combined, then add oil, cheese, and salt to taste, and process until mixture resembles a thick, smooth sauce.
6. Stir half the pistou into soup, and serve the rest on the side. Additional grated Parmesan may also be served as a garnish.

Note: You can use canned beans, though the flavor will not be as intense. Skip step 1, and add drained beans after the potatoes in step 3. You will need to add more water to cover the vegetables.

There are about sixty species of the sunflower: some are annuals, some perennials; they can grow to three feet or fifteen, with heads dainty or a foot across, yellow-petaled (of course), red, or purple. Native to the Great Plains, they are easy to grow, wanting only decent soil and sunshine.

"The more silverware on the table when you sit down, the more fun it is," says Martha. *"You get to try to figure out what you're going to have."*

Etiquette books—especially the old ones—are full of arcane, complex rules governing the placement and use of cutlery. This makes for an excellent party game (if one wishes to take this notion further, Miss Manners' Guide to Excruciatingly Correct Behavior *will provide plenty of ideas). For practical purposes, however, there is only one convention of American table setting to remember: silverware is placed on the table in the order it will be used, from the outside in. The fork for the first course is the farthest to the left; the knife that goes with it is the farthest to the right. Any spoons needed before dessert go among the knives. Dessert silverware rests horizontally above the plate or is brought in later.*

Martha's eclectic table-setting style extends to her flatware. She mixes patterns and periods, avoiding chaos only by maintaining a single level of formality. "I probably wouldn't mix Bakelite dinerware with ornate Victorian silver," she says. *"And I pay attention to proportion and texture."*

•dinner elements

1. Good company comes first.

2. Martha loves to set a busy table: here she mingles half a dozen flatware patterns. Note that none of the monograms are hers—all these pieces were picked up in odd lots at various tag sales, auctions, and consignment shops.

3. Connecticut ivy stands in for Provençal grapevines.

4. Cheeses made of goat's milk and ewe's milk are indigenous to the region. Some may be soaked in cognac or eau-de-vie and wrapped in chestnut leaves; others are rolled in herbs, ash, peppercorns, or pungent tapenade.

5. With the table all cleared, Martha presents the last course.

6. Hand-painted, unglazed soup bowls and dinner plates are separated by plain, glazed Buffalo soup plates in a complementary color. The tablecloth was a happy accident: it's a length of Fortuny fabric whose colors and leafy pattern just happened to match the china.

7. A simple desssert: whole peaches were poached in dry white wine with sugar and a cinnamon stick. Plums, apricots, and most stone fruits take well to the same treatment; choose firm, unblemished fruit, leave unpeeled, and simmer until the fruit is just tender, 5 to 30 minutes, depending on its ripeness.

8. Cool stone is the stuff of farmhouses in the south of France.

COUNTRY STYLE LEG OF LAMB

Lamb is a favorite Mediterranean meat. Fresh rosemary is a natural marinade ingredient; we added thyme and used balsamic vinegar for a flavorful alternative to the more traditional red-wine vinegar.

TO SERVE 8

    1 6- to 8-pound leg of lamb, bone in
    6 garlic cloves, peeled and sliced
      Fresh rosemary
      Fresh thyme
      Salt and freshly ground pepper
    2 bunches parsley
1½ cups balsamic vinegar

1. Heat oven to 400°. Trim fat on lamb to ¼-inch thickness. Cut small, random incisions in the fat and insert garlic and herbs. Sprinkle with salt and pepper. Put lamb fat side up in a roasting pan, place in oven, and cook for 30 minutes.

2. Using a mortar and pestle, crush the parsley, then combine with vinegar. Pour over lamb and continue to cook, ½ hour more for very rare (120° on a meat thermometer), or longer to taste (125° for rare, 130° for medium rare).

APPLE TART

It is important to slice the apples that are used on top as thinly as possible. A mandoline makes this chore a breeze; peel and cut the apples into quarters before slicing.

TO MAKE ONE 12-INCH TART

    1 12-inch Pâte Sucrée Crust (see page 22)
    4 pounds Granny Smith apples, peeled, cored, and quartered, plus 3 apples for garnish
    3 tablespoons unsalted butter
    2 tablespoons sugar, plus additional for garnish
    3 tablespoons plus 1 teaspoon fresh lemon juice
    3 tablespoons plus 1 teaspoon brandy
    2 tablespoons unsalted butter, melted
  ½ cup apricot jam

1. Make Pâte Sucrée Crust as directed and let cool.

2. Heat oven to 250°. Place apple quarters in a shallow roasting pan with the butter, sugar, and 3 tablespoons each lemon juice and brandy. Cook for 2½ hours, stirring occasionally.

3. Pass through a food mill or puree in a food processor. Spread in tart shell. Peel the 3 remaining apples, slice very thin, and arrange on top of puree.

4. Heat the broiler. Protect rim of tart with foil. Brush apples lightly with melted butter and sprinkle with sugar. Place on middle oven rack and broil until apple slices are brown and translucent, about 5 to 10 minutes.

5. In a small pan over low heat, combine apricot jam with the 1 teaspoon lemon juice and 1 teaspoon brandy. Strain if lumpy. Brush over top of tart and serve warm or at room temperature.

> ### { Points of presentation
>
> *Hearty food should not look crude. French cooks know the importance of appealing to eye as well as taste buds even for everyday meals, and will automatically trim a leg of lamb so it looks like a garden, or spend time arranging apple slices on a tart to resemble the petals of a flower.*

THE FIRST APPLE HARVEST is a special occasion, to be marked every year with a celebratory apple tart. This one was made with Granny Smiths, but any crisp, sharp variety of apple would do.

all hallow's eve

potluck supper
& *carving pumpkins*

cold seafood salad
shallot and artichoke tarts
braised veal shanks
with
polenta and salsa verde

pear bread pudding

} 12

THE JACK O'LANTERN
need not be a round orange
head. We made a harlequin
lantern from a Blue Hubbard
squash by carving every
second diamond just half-way
through the flesh.

•perfect potluck

Potluck meals, those where each guest brings a dish, tend to be somewhat casual. Wondering if one could give an elegant potluck dinner party, we borrowed a house in Los Angeles from food writer Merrill Shindler, and asked the chefs and owners of several Los Angeles restaurants to bring their favorite impromptu dishes. The result was a wonderful evening, with good food, conversation, and entertainment, as the chefs traded recipes and ideas.

1. Stacy Dalgleish and Piero Selvaggio came from Valentino.

2. A Roseville vase and Frankoma jug are part of the hosts' vast pottery collection.

3. Mark Peel, the chef of Campanile, waits for La Brea Bakery's Nancy Silverton to slice one of her breads.

4. The open flow of the International Style house, built in the 1940s, makes it perfect for parties.

5. One-month-old Michela dozes while dad Jean-Louis De Mori of Ca' Brea works in the kitchen.

6. Hostess Deborah Sroloff and Martha get comfortable.

7. A virtual wall of windows in the living room provides plenty of light to keep flowers in bloom.

8. Make sure there is an impressive finale to your potluck; for ours, Michael Richard of Citus made his pear bread pudding.

{ A potluck history

Some of the most interesting meals and dishes in American history were born as potluck events. What, after all, was the first Thanksgiving feast but a potluck supper? The pilgrims served what they had on hand. Chief Massasoit and his fellow Wampanoag brought their favorite dishes: oysters, eel, goose, venison, and popcorn (but apparently no turkey).

Food writer Merrill Shindler has given some memorable potlucks. One bore the theme "Foods of Your Childhood": people who normally lunch on napoleon of squid and rosemary sorbet dined, instead, on Ring Dings, Mallomars, Yankee Doodles, Jell-O, Twinkies, and Sno Balls. One guest, a restaurant critic with a refined palate, arrived with a pot of canned spaghetti tossed with butter and ketchup. A psychiatrist brought banana, mayonnaise, and peanut-butter sandwiches sprinkled with brown sugar. Another guest brought his mother, who made tuna surprise.

A great potluck was born when an ancient avocado tree in a friend's yard was overwhelmed with fruit. Guests picked all they wanted, and returned later with an avocado dish of their choosing. There were a few guacamoles, but also pies and quiches, a wonderful cold soup flavored with dill, a daiquiri and a margarita (both tasted better than we'd thought possible), and a mousse in which the avocado was whipped with Chartreuse, sugar, and cream and then returned to its shell. It was one of the most fattening potlucks of all time, but just goes to prove that the theme's the thing.

FORTIES CHINA complements the colors of the house.

COLD SEAFOOD SALAD

This salad is typical of the delicious Venetian cooking Antonio Tommasi and Jean-Louis De Mori serve at Ca' Brea.

TO SERVE 4

  1 each red and yellow peppers
 12 black mussels, scrubbed and debearded
 12 manila clams, scrubbed
 12 medium bay scallops, rinsed, with
     muscles removed
 12 medium shrimp, peeled and deveined
  6 ounces calamari, cut into strips
 ½ cup extra-virgin olive oil
 ¼ cup fresh lemon juice
  2 teaspoons chopped garlic
 ¼ teaspoon red-pepper flakes

   Salt and freshly ground pepper
  6 marinated artichoke hearts
 ½ cup chopped black olives
  1 tablespoon chopped fresh basil leaves

1. Roast peppers under a broiler until blackened. Cool in a paper bag. Peel and seed peppers, and cut into strips. Set aside.
2. Poach seafood separately in simmering salted water. Cook mussels and clams until shells open, 5 to 7 minutes. Cook scallops, shrimp, and calamari until opaque, 5 to 7 minutes. Discard any unopened mussels and clams. Drain all seafood and let cool; set aside.
3. In a small bowl, whisk together oil, lemon juice, garlic, red-pepper flakes, and salt and pepper to taste.
4. In a large serving bowl, combine cooled seafood (keep mussels and clams in their shells), pepper strips, artichoke hearts, olives, and basil. Add dressing and mix thoroughly. Serve immediately.

SHALLOT AND ARTICHOKE TARTS

Serve in wedges as an appetizer, or serve whole, with soup or salad, as a light lunch.

TO MAKE FOUR 4-INCH TARTS

4 medium artichokes (about 2 pounds)

¼ cup plus 2 tablespoons olive oil

3 teaspoons fresh lemon juice

Salt and freshly ground pepper

1½ pounds shallots (about 30), peeled and thinly sliced

½ pound frozen all-butter puff pastry, thawed in refrigerator

1 egg yolk beaten with 1 teaspoon water, for egg wash

Mark Peel's Pesto (recipe follows)

1. Cut away leaves of artichokes, leaving the hearts. Scoop out and discard chokes. Cut each heart in half lengthwise. Place in a steamer basket set in a large saucepan filled with 2 to 3 inches of water. Bring to a boil, lower heat, cover, and steam until hearts are barely tender, about 15 minutes. Refresh in ice water, drain well, and dry thoroughly. Cut each half into 8 wedges.

2. In a medium bowl, whisk together 2 tablespoons of the olive oil, the lemon juice, and salt and pepper to taste. Carefully stir in artichoke hearts, making sure they are thoroughly coated. Let marinate until ready to use.

3. In a large skillet, heat remaining ¼ cup olive oil over medium heat. Add shallots and cook, covered, just until tender, 6 to 7 minutes. Do not allow to brown. Spread on a platter to cool.

4. Roll out puff pastry to ⅛ inch, and cut out four circles 5 inches in diameter. Fold in ½-inch edge, pleating as you go along, and place on parchment-lined baking sheets. Refrigerate for 30 minutes.

5. Heat oven to 375°. Remove shells from refrigerator. To assemble tarts, spread shallots on shells, making a layer about ¼ inch thick and leaving a border of about ¼ inch. Arrange artichoke wedges on top of shallots. Brush edges of dough with egg wash. Bake until crust is golden brown and shallots are lightly colored, about 15 minutes. Serve immediately, drizzled with Mark Peel's Pesto.

Individual tarts are delicious and portable potluck fare.

MARK PEEL'S PESTO

This pesto adds a nice flavor and color to the Shallot and Artichoke Tarts.

TO MAKE ½ CUP

3 cloves garlic

3 tablespoons lightly toasted pine nuts

½ teaspoon kosher salt, plus more to taste

¼ cup plus 1 tablespoon extra-virgin olive oil

1 cup coarsely chopped and loosely packed basil leaves

Lemon juice

Using a mortar and pestle, crush garlic and pine nuts with salt and 1 tablespoon of the oil until pulverized. Add basil leaves and work until you have a rough paste. Blend in remaining olive oil in a stream. Add more salt, and lemon juice to taste.

bRAISED VEAL SHANKS

At the restaurant Campanile, this dish is served with triangles of
Polenta (see recipe, page 42) and Salsa Verde (recipe follows).

TO SERVE 6 TO 8

  2 whole veal shanks, about 3½ pounds each
⅓ cup plus 3 tablespoons olive oil
½ teaspoon juniper berries
½ teaspoon whole black peppercorns
6-7 sprigs fresh thyme
6-7 sprigs fresh rosemary
  1 tablespoon salt
¾ teaspoon freshly ground pepper
  1 green cabbage, cored and cut into 2-inch-thick slices
  1 large onion, cut into 2-inch chunks
  3 large carrots, cut into 2-inch-long sticks
  5 large celery stalks, peeled and cut into 2-inch-long pieces
  2 large leeks, whites only, trimmed and cut into 2-inch-long strips
  1 medium fennel bulb trimmed and cut into ⅛-inch-thick slices
  1 cup dry white wine
  2 tablespoons white-wine vinegar
  5 cups good-quality, low-salt beef stock
  5 cups water
  2 heads garlic
  4 sprigs fresh parsley

1. Mix together ⅓ cup of the olive oil, the juniper berries, peppercorns, and several sprigs each of thyme and rosemary. Marinate
veal shanks in mixture at least 8 hours, or refrigerate up to 2 days.
2. Heat the grill, and heat oven to 450°. Discard marinade. Season
shanks with salt and pepper; grill until brown, about 10 minutes.
3. While shanks are browning, heat remaining 3 tablespoons oil in
a large, ovenproof casserole over medium heat. Sauté vegetables
until brown on all sides, about 10 minutes. Deglaze pan with wine
and vinegar, and reduce by about a quarter. Add stock, water, garlic, remaining thyme and rosemary, and parsley; bring to a simmer.
4. When shanks are brown, transfer to casserole with vegetables
and place in oven. Braise, uncovered, until shanks are tender,
about 2 hours. Turn shanks every 30 minutes.
5. Serve as described in the caption, above right.

*To serve the veal shanks, cut meat lengthwise from bone;
garnish platter with vegetables, polenta triangles, salsa
verde, and shank bones stood on end.*

SALSA VERDE

TO MAKE ABOUT ¾ CUP

  3 anchovy fillets, chopped
  3 large garlic cloves, chopped
  1 tablespoon plus 1 teaspoon capers
¾ cup extra-virgin olive oil
  2 tablespoons fresh lemon juice
  3 tablespoons chopped fresh flat-leaf parsley leaves
  2 tablespoons each chopped fresh basil, marjoram, and mint
    Salt and freshly ground pepper

1. Mash anchovies, garlic, and capers to a paste with 2 tablespoons
of the oil. Stir in lemon juice and remaining oil.
2. When ready to serve, stir in chopped herbs and season with salt
and pepper. Use within 2 hours.

TRUMPET LILIES
(*Lilium longiflorum*),
native to Formosa and the
Ryukuy islands, are
widely cultivated for their
large, fragrant pure white
funnel-form flowers.

PEAR BREAD PUDDING

Michel Richard of Citrus likes to use brioche in this homey dessert.

TO SERVE 10 TO 12

- 13 Bartlett pears, peeled
- 1 bottle champagne or dry white wine
- 1 cup sugar
- 8 slices fresh brioche or white bread, crusts removed
- 2 cups milk
- 2 cups heavy cream
- 3 large eggs
- ⅔ cup brown sugar
- ½ teaspoon ground coriander
  Pinch of salt
  Caramel Sauce
- ½ cup granulated sugar
- 2 tablespoons fresh lemon juice
- 1 cup milk
- 1 cup pear-poaching liquid

1. In a large saucepan over medium heat, combine champagne and sugar. Bring mixture to a boil and cook for 5 minutes. Add 12 of the pears, lower heat, and cook until tender, 20 to 30 minutes. Transfer pears and liquid to a bowl and refrigerate overnight.

2. Heat oven to 325°. Line a 10-by-2-inch round ovenproof glass dish with plastic wrap. Remove pears from poaching liquid; reserve liquid. Core and quarter poached pears; thinly slice lengthwise, but don't separate slices. Arrange on pan bottom. Place bread slices in two overlapping layers on top.

3. In a medium bowl, whisk together milk, cream, eggs, brown sugar, coriander, and salt. Pour over bread slices.

4. Place baking dish in a pan filled with enough boiling water to reach halfway up sides of dish. Cover pan with foil; bake for 1 hour.

5. Cool completely and unmold pudding onto a serving plate. Discard plastic wrap. Refrigerate pudding until ready to serve.

6. To make Caramel Sauce, heat sugar and lemon juice in a heavy, medium saucepan over low heat until mixture turns deep amber. Carefully stir in milk and pear-poaching liquid; boil for 1 minute, until smooth. Strain and use immediately.

7. To serve pudding, cut into slices, inserting slices of remaining Bartlett pear. Serve with Caramel Sauce.

{ **Dinner-table rules**

A potluck meal put together on site can be a delightful way for friends to entertain each other, but only with some basic agreement to avoid culinary chaos.

A host or coordinator must assign a course to each guest and ascertain that the dishes won't clash—too much. Each guest should be told about oven type and capacity and about refrigerator space; guests in turn must warn the host about any special serving requirements. Don't forget to arrange kitchen cleanup, and appoint one guest to provide drinks. At our party, Martha drew this duty.

Dessert was a surprise gift } *Warm caramel sauce laps at pear bread pudding garnished with thinly sliced Bartlett pears.*

•art of carving

1. The right tools for the job: serrated blades for carving, wood chisels and melon ballers to leave behind a layer of translucent flesh, and utility knives to clean rough edges.

2. Pick any squash and let its shape and color inspire you.

3. Draw the design you plan to carve on a sheet of paper, then tape the drawing to the gourd and "trace" the design with pushpin pricks.

4. Colored waxed paper tacked to the inside of the "windows" creates the stained-glass effect.

5. If Michelangelo's "David" can lurk inside every block of marble, why not a Martian in every squash?

The word "pumpkin" has no botanical meaning. In Latin, the genus is Cucurbita; in English, squash—the proper word for all we think of as pumpkins, gourds, and (obviously) squash. "I hate the word 'pumpkin,' " says Glenn Drowns, of Caklamus, Iowa, who has grown them since the age of seven and has about 650 varieties in his seed collection. "Botanically, they're all squash."

Cucurbita has twenty recorded species, four of them still in cultivation. C. maxima includes the largest fruits in the plant kingdom—contest winners of more than eight hundred pounds. C. moschata, a very good keeper, is the sweetest-flavored species; it typically has a hard, ridged stem that flares where it attaches to the fruit and thick, dark-orange flesh. C. pepo includes summer squash, acorns, Delicatas, and the orange field pumpkins so familar from October porches. The least grown species, C. argyrosperma is harder to identify; it prefers southern climates and has the best drought tolerance.

THE PHOTOGRAPHERS

WILLIAM ABRANOWICZ
pages 2, 8 (second from top), 28-33, 106, 114 (top row; bottom left), 126, 136, 137.

RUVÉN AFANADOR
pages 8 (top), 14, 24, 25.

DAVIES AND STARR
pages 8 (third from bottom), 50.

TODD EBERLE
pages 8 (third from top), 86, 87, 98-105.

MICHAEL GRIMM
page 108 (bottom).

GUZMAN
page 11.

RUEDI HOFMANN
pages 8 (second from bottom), 116-125.

THIBAULT JEANSON
pages 90, 92-97.

JON JENSEN
pages 44-48, 51.

TED MORRISON
pages 26, 36, 37.

VICTORIA PEARSON
*front cover, back cover (left), pages 1, 5, 6, 8 (bottom), 9 (top; third from bottom; bottom), 13,
66-85, 86 (bottom left), 108-113, 114 (middle; bottom center and right), 115, 128-135.*

GRANT PETERSON
back cover, pages 8 (second from bottom),16-23, 35, 54-65.

CHRIS SANDERS
pages 52, 53.

WILLIAM WALDRON
pages 8 (second from top), 88, 91, 123 (top row, second from right).

BRUCE WOLF
pages 8 (third from top), 38-43.

THE GUIDE

NEW YEAR'S DAY

page 14

American **matte-white roadside pottery**, $28, and **fluted florist vase**, $35, *both at U.S.E.D., 17 Perry Street, New York, NY 10014; 212-627-0730.*

pages 16, 19 to 21, 23

Kent Irish **handkerchief linen** (for tablecloth and napkins), $18 to $20 per yard, *from Hamilton Adams Linen. Call 212-221-0800 for retailers.*

pages 19 to 21

Octagonal creamware **bowl**, $2,500 for 54-piece set, *at Lucullus, 610 Chartres Street, New Orleans, LA 70130; 504-528-9620.*

page 20

French faience **tureen** and **ladle**, $1,875 for complete service, *at Lucullus, 610 Chartres Street, New Orleans, LA 70130; 504-528-9620.*

page 21

Green George III **armchairs** (set of six), *at Kentshire Galleries, 37 East 12th Street, New York, NY 10003; 212-673-6644. Price upon request.* Kent Irish **handkerchief linen** (for curtain), $18 to $20 per yard, *from Hamilton Adams Linen. Call 212-221-0800 for retailers.* Old-fashioned **pearl buttons** (on curtain), $2 each, *at Tender Buttons, 143 East 62nd Street, New York, NY 10021; 212-758-7004.*

page 23

Empire Creil creamware **dessert plate**, $2,500 for 54-piece set, *at Lucullus, 610 Chartres Street, New Orleans, LA 70130; 504-528-9620.*

page 24

Special thanks to Stonecrop Nursery, Cold Spring, NY. To mail-order branches, call Maria Babick at International Garden, 807 Sixth Avenue, New York, NY 10001; 212-929-9418.
1. American **matte-gray vase**, $85, *at Fritz's American Wonder at the Tomato Factory, 2 Somerset Street, Hopewell, NJ 08525; 609-466-9833.* Bulbous **matte-green roadside vase**, $45, *at U.S.E.D., 17 Perry Street, New York, NY 10014; 212-627-0730.* 3. American matte-green **wall pocket**, $75, *at Fritz's American Wonder at the Tomato Factory, see above.*

page 26

Antique **molds**, *at Diane Cazalet, 26340 Alexander Place, Los Altos, CA 94022; 415-949-0560.* Striated **heart mold**, $38, *at La Cuisine, 800-521-1176.*

page 28

Wedgwood blue-and-puce-bordered **dessert plates**, $800 per pair, *at Bardith Ltd., 901 Madison Avenue, New York, NY 10021; 212-737-3775.*

page 29

Late Victorian cranberry **bulb vase**, $565, *at James II Galleries Ltd., 11 East 57th Street, 4th floor, New York, NY 10022; 212-355-7040.* **White-truffle oil**, from $16 (55 milliliters) to $45 (255 milliliters), *at Balducci's, 212-673-2600 or (outside NYC) 800-822-1444.* Lollo rossa, red oak, and red romaine **baby lettuces**, from $4.75 (half pound) to $8.50 (one pound), *at Fines Herbes Co., 800-231-9022. Half-pound minimum; other varieties available.*

pages 29, 31, 33

Barr Flight Barr Worcester **dinner plates**, $550 per pair, English **cut-glass flutes**, $250 for 2, *all at Bardith Ltd., 901 Madison Avenue, New York, NY 10021; 212-737-3775.* Nineteenth-century **champagne flutes**, $1,150 for 7, *at James II Galleries Ltd., 11 East 57th Street, 4th floor, New York, NY 10022; 212-355-7040.*

page 31

Nineteenth-century Aubusson-covered **salon chair**, $26,000 for set of 4 with love seat, *at Morgan Gallery, Place des Antiquaires, 125 East 57th Street, New York, NY 10022; 212-644-7000.* Organic free-range **poussins** (young chickens), $5 each, *at D'Artagnan, 800-327-8246.*

pages 31 and 33

Molded-glass **candlesticks**, $635, *at James II Galleries Ltd., 11 East 57th Street, 4th floor, New York, NY 10022; 212-355-7040.*

page 32

Four-quart Pillivuyt **soufflé dish**, $12.50, *at Dean & Deluca Inc., 212-431-1691, ext. 223 or 270, or (outside NYC) 800-221-7714.*

pages 34 to 37

Callebaut chocolate (all varieties), *at the Annex Cookery, 5526 Walnut Street, Pittsburgh, PA 15232; 413-621-6215.* **Valrhona chocolate** (all varieties), *at the Chocolate Gallery, 34 West 22nd Street, New York, NY 10010; 212-675-2253; and La Cuisine, 800-521-1176.*

page 36

Italian **edible gold leaf,** $40 for 25 sheets, OMC Atlas **pasta machine,** $52, *both at La Cuisine, 800-521-1176.*

page 37

Plastic **pear molds,** $25 to $40, *at La Cuisine, 800-521-1176.*

EASTER SUNDAY

pages 40, 42, 43

Ecru **linen with celadon appliqué,** linen **dinner napkins,** linen **cocktail napkins,** antique sterling **napkin ring,** *all at the Grand Acquisitor, 110 North Main Street, East Hampton, NY 11937; 516-324-7272. Appointment suggested; prices upon request.*

page 41

Ecru **linen with Cluny-lace border,** *at the Grand Acquisitor, 110 North Main Street, East Hampton, NY 11937; 516-324-7272. Appointment suggested; price upon request.*

pages 42, 43

French **dinner knives,** $150 for set of 10, *at Consignmart, 877 Post Road East, Westport, CT 06880; 203-226-0841.* **Flower arrangements** *by Beth White, 20 Surrey Court, East Hampton, NY 11937; 516-324-9239.*

page 43

Ateco paste **food coloring,** $1.15 to $1.99 per 1-ounce jar, Odense **marzipan,** $3.29 for 7 ounces, *both at the Chocolate Gallery, 34 West 22nd Street, New York, NY 10010; 212-675-2253.*

A FINE SPRING DAY

pages 44 to 51

Salad-green sources: *Malibu Farms Inc., the City Market, 953 South San Pedro Street, Los Angeles, CA 90015; 213-622-4372. Free catalog. Solviva, Box 582 RFD, Vineyard Haven, MA 02568; 508-693-3341. From $12 per pound.* **Herb sources:** *Fines Herbes, 800-231-9022. Malibu Farms Inc., see above.*

page 48

Shiitake mushrooms, $19 for one-pound box, $28 for two-pound box, *at Delftree Farm, 800-243-3742. One-pound minimum order.*

pages 52, 53

Seed sources: *W. Atlee Burpee & Co., 300 Park Avenue, Warminster, PA 18974; 215-674-4900. Free catalog. The Cook's Garden, Box 535, Londonderry, VT 05148; 802-824-3400. Catalog, $1. Gurney's Seed Nursery, 110 Capitol Street, Yankton, SD 57079; 605-665-1930. Free catalog. Park Seed Co., 800-845-3369. Free catalog. Thompson & Morgan, Box 1308, Jackson, NJ 08527; 908-363-2225 or 800-274-7333 (outside NJ). Free*

catalog. **Potting soil,** *available at home and garden centers nationwide.* Biodegradable **Peat Pots** by Jiffy, *from about 99¢ for 12, at Gurney's Seed Nursery and Burpee's (see above).* "Plug" **seed-starting trays,** $6.50 for 54 cells, *at Park Seed and Burpee's (see above).*

page 53

Plastic **pot and garden labels,** $2.95 for 100, *at W. Atlee Burpee & Co., 300 Park Avenue, Warminster, PA 18974; 215-674-4900. Free catalog.* Etched zinc **flower and plant markers,** $8 for 25, *at Smith & Hawken, 25 Corte Madera, Mill Valley, CA 94941; 415-383-2000.*

MOTHER'S DAY

pages 54, 60, 61

Edible pansies, $7.87 for tray of 50, *at Malibu Farms Inc., The City Market, 953 South San Pedro Street, Los Angeles, CA 90015; 213-622-4372; and MaxiFlowers a la Carte; 800-995-6294. Call for availability and prices.*

page 56

Hepplewhite **shield-back chair** (circa 1770), $53,500 for set of 8, *at Kentshire Galleries Ltd., 37 East 12th Street, New York, NY 10003; 212-673-6644.*

page 61

Ateco paste **food coloring,** $1.15 to $1.99 per 1-ounce jar, *at the Chocolate Gallery, 34 West 22nd Street, New York, NY 10010; 212-675-2253.*

pages 61, 63, 64

10" **pastry bag,** $1.49, *at the Chocolate Gallery, 34 West 22nd Street, New York, NY 10010; 212-675-2253.*

page 64

Offset icing spatula, from $2.19 (3½" blade) to $5.99 (8" blade); 3"-tall heart-shaped cake **pans,** from $15.99 (5" pan) to $17.99 (8" pan); *all at the Chocolate Gallery, 34 West 22nd Street, New York, NY 10010; 212-675-2253.*

SUMMER GARDEN PARTY

pages 68 to 75

Flowers *by Steve Rubin/Paper White; 212-675-3599.*

pages 66, 68

10"-round **paper lantern,** $4.50, *at Phoenix Emport Inc., 51 Mott Street, New York, NY 10013; 212-608-6670.*

page 67

Century Sportsman cast-iron **outdoor cooker,** $89.99, *at Gracious Home, 1220 Third Avenue, New York, NY 10021; 212-517-6300. Also at Ace Hardware stores nationwide.*

page 68

Lighting *by Frost Lighting Inc., Box 489, FDR Station, New York, NY 10150; 212-751-0223; and Frost Lighting Co. of Illinois Inc., Box 750, Glenview, IL 60025; 708-729-8200.* White cotton **apron**, $6.95, *at OK Uniform Co. Inc., 507 Broadway, New York, NY 10012; 212-966-1984.*

pages 68, 75

10'-by-10' white **canopy tents**, *at Starr Tents, 800-466-4811.*

pages 68, 69

White wooden **folding chairs**, and **maize tablecloths**, *both at Party Rental Ltd. Call 212-594-8510 for information.* Silk organza **table topper** *sewn by the Festive Touch, 1771 Post Road East, #314, Westport, CT 06880; 203-330-0719.* Pale-yellow **silk organza**, $11.95 per yard, *at Rosen & Chadick Textiles, 246 West 40th Street, New York, NY 10018; 212-869-0136.*

pages 68, 70, 71

Chopsticks, wooden skewers, and Asian ingredients, *at Oriental Food Market and Cooking School, 2801 West Howard, Chicago, IL 60645; 312-274-2826. Send $2 for catalog and price list.*

page 70

Bamboo **steamers**, $26.95 for 10" round, $29.95 for 12" round, *both at Kam Kuo Food Corp., 7 Mott Street, New York, NY 10013; 212-349-3097.*

FIRST DAY OF SUMMER

Special thanks to Thomas Callaway and Janece Doty Word of Thomas Callaway Bench Works Inc., 2920 Nebraska Avenue, Santa Monica, CA 90404; 310-828-9379.

pages 78, 79

Dempster hand-woven cotton **napkins** in assorted colors, $4.50, *at Montana Mercantile, 1500 Montana Avenue, Santa Monica, CA 90403; 213-451-1418.*

pages 80, 81, and 83

Hand-wrought-iron Butterfly **grill**, $225; hand-wrought-iron Tiki **fork**, $100; *both at Mildred, Box 661365, Los Angeles, CA 90066; 310-305-1218.*

pages 50, 53, and 55

Mexican glass **tumbler**, $3.95, *at Maison et Café American Rag Compagnie, 148 South La Brea Avenue, Los Angeles, CA 90036; 213-935-3157.*

pages 86, 87

Special thanks to Mark Viette of André Viette Farm and Nursery, Route 1, Box 16, Fishersville, VA 22939; 703-943-2315; and Steve Frowine of White Flower Farm, Box 50, Litchfield, CT 06759; 203-496-9600. **Poppy seeds** *at the Cook's Garden, Box 535, Londonderry, VT 05148; 802-824-3400;*

Park Seed Co.; 800-845-3369; Thompson & Morgan; 800-274-7333. **Poppy seedlings** *at Van Bourgondien & Sons, Box 1000, 245 Farmingdale Road, Babylon, NY 11702; 516-669-3520; Wayside Gardens; 800-845-1124; White Flower Farm, Box 50, Litchfield, CT 06759; 203-496-9600.*

A WEDDING AT HOME

page 90

Wedding cake, $4 per person, *from the Cupcake Café, 522 Ninth Avenue, New York, NY 10018; 212-465-1530.* Bromley Hall **toile** (#50152.01, used for tablecloth), *from Brunschwig & Fils Inc., 979 Third Avenue, New York, NY 10022; 212-838-7878. To the trade only.*

pages 90, 92-97

Catering *by Paula LeDuc Fine Catering, 1350 Park Avenue, Emeryville, CA 94608; 510-547-7825.*

page 91

Flowers *designed by Beth White, 20 Surrey Court, East Hampton, NY 11937; 516-324-9239.* **Ribbons**, *from $2 per yard, at Hyman Hendler & Sons, 67 West 38th Street, New York, NY 10018; 212-840-8393.* **Flower shears,** $16, and galvanized-steel **buckets**, *from $19.50 (for 8") to $24.40 (for 16"), all at Smith & Hawken, 25 Corte Madera, Mill Valley, CA 94941; 415-383-2000.* **Mail-order flowers** *at Calyx & Corolla, 800-877-7836.*

page 94

Hartland glass **cake plate**, $155, *from Simon Pearce, 500 Park Avenue, New York, NY 10022; 212-421-8801.*

page 94

Edible flowers *at MaxiFlowers a la Carte; 800-995-6294. Call for availability and prices. Also at Malibu Farms Inc., The City Market, 953 South San Pedro Street, Los Angeles, CA 90015; 213-622-4372.*

FOURTH OF JULY

Travel arrangements courtesy of Delta Air Lines. Special thanks to Cumberland Island National Seashore, Box 806, St. Marys, GA 31558; and the Greyfield Inn, 4 North Second Street, Fernindina, FL 32034; 904-261-6408.

page 100

2½-gallon **mason jar** by Libby, $23, *at Wooden Indian, 60 West 15th Street, New York, NY 10011; 212-243-8590.*

pages 100, 103, 104

Blue-rimmed plate, $15, **mug**, $9, **bowl**, $10, *all at Ashling, 517 Sutter Street, San Francisco, CA 94102; 415-986-8663.*

page 106

Orbit **candle lantern with citronella**, $13.95, *at the Everyday Gardener, 2947-A Old Canton Road, Jackson, MS 39216; 601-981-0273.*

pages 108, 114, 115

Tent *custom-sewn by Martin Izquierdo Studios, 118 West 22nd Street, 9th floor, New York, NY 10011; 212-807-9757.* **Cotton scrim** (used for canopy), $1 per yard, plus $5 cutting fee, *at Rose Brand, 517 West 35th Street, New York, NY 10001; 212-594-7424.* 10' by 10' **tent frame**, $195, *at Partytime Tents & Canopies, Box 644, Branchville, NJ 07826; 201-948-2426.*

pages 108 to 110, 112 to 115

Painted tablecloth and napkins *designed by Bette Blau Designs, 1 Astor Place, New York, NY 10003; 212-982-3509.* Medium-weight **cotton muslin**, $4.55 per yard, plus $5 cutting fee, *at Rose Brand, 517 West 35th Street, New York, NY 10001; 212-594-7424.* DEKA-Permanent **fabric paint**, from $2.25, Liquitex Acrylic Concentrated **Artist's Color**, from $2.50, *both at craft and art-supply stores nationwide.*

pages 108, 109, 112

China-clam shell, $18.50, **Murex ramosus**, $25, **medium starfish**, $2.50, **small starfish**, $1.50, *all at The Shell Cellar, South Street Seaport, 89 South Street, New York, NY 10038; 212-962-1076.*

page 111

Spanish **saffron**, $16 for 2-gram jar, *at Williams-Sonoma stores nationwide. Call 800-541-1262 for nearest location.*

page 113

Hand-held **salamander**, $8, *at Williams-Sonoma stores nationwide. Call 800-541-1262 for nearest location.*

page 114

Star lantern, $30, *at La Luz de Jesus Gallery, 7400 Melrose Avenue, 2nd floor, Los Angeles, CA 90046; 213-651-4875.* **Wire rings**, from 20¢ each (8" diameter), **florist's wire**, $3 per spool, *both at New York Florists' Supply Co., 103 West 28th Street, New York, NY 10001; 212-564-6086.* Hanging glass **votive-candle holders**, $2.50 each, *at Jim Henry Enterprises; 800-448-3263.* 4' Tag **citronella torch**, $7.50, *at the Everyday Gardener, 2947-A Old Canton Road, Jackson, MS 39216; 601-981-0273.* **Beachcomber torches**, $5.97 to $9.97, *at Lamplight Farms, 4900 North Lilly Road, Menomonee Falls, WI 53051; 414-781-9590.*

page 118

Fresh crayfish, from 40¢ to $1.95 per pound (in season February/March to July), **aquaculture and soft-shell crayfish**, from $7.50 to $9 per pound, **quick-frozen cooked varieties**, $2.50 per pound (available year-round), *all at Louisiana Seafood Exchange, 428 Jefferson Highway, Jefferson, LA 70121; 504-834-9393.*

page 122

Lucrezia **fabric** (used for tablecloth) by Fortuny, $247.50 per yard, *at Fortuny Inc., 509 Madison Avenue, New York, NY 10022; 212-753-7153.* Tuscan **dinner plate**, $60, and **soup bowl**, $24, both by Aletha Soulé for the Loom Company, *at Bergdorf Goodman, 754 Fifth Avenue, New York, NY 10019; 212-753-7300. Also at Mixt, 1811 South Catalina Avenue, Redondo Beach, CA 90277; 212-375-3665; and Javier Puig, 118 North Fourth Street, Minneapolis, MN 55401; 612-332-6001.* 24" hem-stitched linen **napkins**, $18 each, *at E. Braun & Co., 717 Madison Avenue, New York, NY 10021; 212-838-0650.* DEKA-Permanent **fabric paint**, from $2.25, *at craft and art-supply stores nationwide.*

page 126

German **waxed tissue paper**, $2.75 per sheet, *at Kate's Paperie, 8 West 13th Street, New York, NY 10011; 212-633-0570.*

pages 127 to 135

Special thanks to Stacy Dalgleish and Piero Selvaggio of Valentino, Mark Peel of Campanile, Michel Richard of Citrus, Nancy Silverton of La Brea Bakery, and Antonio Tommasi and Jean-Louis De Mori of Ca' Brea.

pages 136, 137

Special thanks to Sara Ruffin, Beth White, and Corey Tippin; Jack Musnicki at Bridgehampton Landscaping, Box 757, Pauls Lane, Bridgehampton, NY 11932; 516-537-0888; the Green Thumb of Water Mill, 829 Montauk Highway, Water Mill, NY 11976; 516-726-1900; and Ron Steinhilber and Sue Calden of the Pink House, 26 James Lane, East Hampton, NY 11937; 516-324-3400. **Blue Hubbard squash**, 40¢ per pound, *at Native Farms, 332 East 11th Street, New York, NY 10003; 212-614-0727.* **Pumpkins**, 29¢ per pounds, *at the Green Thumb of Water Mill, see above.*

page 136

Mini orange-handled tools and **stencils** by Pumpkin Carving, $12.98, *at Lillian Vernon; 800-285-5555.* **Wood-carving tools** by Loew-Cornell, $9.50, *at Pearl Paint; 800-451-6327.* **X-Acto knife**, $2.69; **X-Acto blade #1**, $1.79 for packet of 5, *both at New York Art Supply; 800-950-6111.* **Saw nest** (mini saw with blade) by Allway, $5.98, utility **masking tape** by 3M, $2.98 per roll, **pushpins** by Moore, $1.98, *all at Barson Hardware Co. Inc., 35 West 44th Street, New York, NY 10036; 212-944-8181.* **Large-handled utility knife** by X-Acto, $4.89, **saw blade** by X-Acto, $4.95 for packet of 5, *both at New York Art Supply, see above.*

INDEX

A

Aïoli 112
Angel Food Sheet Cake 60
Apple Tart 124
Artichoke and Shallot Tarts 131
Asparagus
  blanched 43
  with basil-tarragon
   dipping sauce 95
  pencil, with tarragon oil 49

B

Baked Stuffed Peaches 84
Basil Aïoli 93
Beef
  fillet balsamico with
   red-onion confit 72
Berry compote, warm 40
Blanched Asparagus 43
Bloody Marys 40
Blueberry Pinwheels 96
Blueberry pie, old fashioned 104
Braised Veal Shanks 132
Bread pudding, pear 134
Buttermilk French Toast 40

C

Caesar Salad 46
Cakes
  angel food 60
  chocolate romance 34

  coconut cloud 63
  pansy layer 60
  raspberry ruffle 64
Caramelized Lemon Tart 22
Carpaccio Teardrops 93
Chicken
  coq au champagne 30
  spicy fried 102
  stock 20, 57
Chocolate Confectionery 36
Chocolate Ganache 34
Chocolate Romance Cake 34
Chocolate soufflé, rich 33
Coconut Cloud Cake 63
Cold Seafood Salad 130
Cold Sesame Noodles 75
Coleslaw, peanut 104
Consommé with
  Herb Dumplings 56
Cookies
  blueberry pinwheels 96
  meringue mushrooms 93
  praline calla lilies with
   lemon cream 96
  violet nosegays 94
Coq au Champagne 30
Country Leg of Lamb 124
Crackers
  flaky Parmesan 16
  grissini 17
Crayfish, deviled 118
Cream Scones 95

D

Deviled Crayfish 118
Dumplings
  herb 57
  seafood 71
  vegetable 71

E

Eggs, poached on
  rounds of polenta 42

F

Fillet of Beef Balsamico
  with Red Onion Confit 72
Fish Soup 18
Fish Stock 18
Flaky Parmesan Crackers 16
Flan 112
Forcing Branches 24
French toast, buttermilk 40
Fresh Pea Soup 20
Fried chicken, spicy 102
Frisée with Sautéed Shrimp,
  Marinated Olives, and Capers 50
Frostings and Fillings
  chocolate ganache 34
  lemon crème fraîche 95
  meringue buttercream 64
  seven-minute icing 63
  vanilla buttercream 61

G

Garden Party Planning 69
Gazpacho, white, with grapes 108
Gougères 28
Granita di Caffé 84
Grill Roasted Vegetables 112
Grilled Mushrooms,
  Fennel, and Peppers 80
Grilled Shiitake Mushrooms
  on Japanese Greens 49
Grilled Shrimp in the Shells 83
Grilled Swiss Chard Packets 81
Grissini 17
Growing Salad Greens 52

H

Heart Salad 29
Herb Beurre Blanc 43
Herb Dumplings 57
Herbed Tomato Salad 47

L

Lamb
  country leg of 124
  navarin of, with
   spring vegetables 58
Lemon Crème Fraîche 95
Lighting, outdoor 114
Linens, vintage 29

M

Mark Peel's Pesto 131
Marzipan Eggs 43
Mashed Potatoes with Sorrel 58
Meringue Buttercream 64
Meringue Mushrooms 93
Meringues 61
Mesclun Salad 49
Mushrooms
  grilled, with fennel
  and peppers 80
  grilled shiitake,
  on Japanese greens 49
Mussels Remoulade 74

N

Navarin of Lamb
  with Spring Vegetables 58
Noodles, cold sesame 75

O

Old-Fashioned Blueberry Pie 104
Outdoor Lighting 114

P

Paella 111
Pansy Layer Cake 60
Parsnip Puree 30
Pastry crusts
  pâte brisée (basic crust) 105
  pâte sucrée (basic sweet crust) 22
Pâte Brisée 105
Pâte Sucrée 22
Peaches, baked and stuffed 84
Peanut Coleslaw 104
Pear Bread Pudding 134
Pearl Balls 70
Pea soup, fresh 20
Pencil Asparagus
  with Tarragon Oil 49
Peppers
  roasted hearts, with
  parsnip puree 30
  roasted red-pepper dip 72
Pesto, Mark Peel's 131
Picnic Packing 100

Pies and tarts
  apple tart 124
  caramelized lemon tart 22
  old-fashioned blueberry pie 104
  shallot and artichoke tarts 131
  torta di riso 83
Pistou Soup 121
Poached Eggs
  on Rounds of Polenta 42
Polenta 42
Poppies 86
Potatoes, mashed with sorrel 58
Praline Calla Lilies
  with Lemon Cream 96
Pumpkins 136

R

Raspberry Ruffle 64
Raspberry Syrup 64
Red Onion Confit 72
Remoulade Sauce 75
Rich Chocolate Soufflé 33
Rice Torte (Torta di Riso) 83
Roasted Pepper Hearts
  with Parsnip Puree 30
Roasted Red Pepper Dip 72
Roasted Vegetable Soup 21
Rouille 18

S

Salad greens, how to grow 52
Salads
  caesar 46
  cold seafood 130
  frisée with sautéed shrimp 50
  grilled shiitake mushrooms
  on Japanese greens 49
  heart 29
  herbed tomato 47
  mesclun 49
  spring, with citrus vinaigrette 46
  stars and strips 103
Salsa Verde 132
Sangria, white 108
Sauces, dips, and dressings
  aïoli 112

basil aïoli 93
  herb beurre blanc 43
  Mark Peel's pesto 131
  red-onion confit 72
  remoulade 75
  roasted red-pepper dip 72
  rouille 18
  salsa verde 132
  spicy dipping sauce 71
  yellow tomato vinaigrette 49
Scones, cream 95
Seafood
  cold salad 130
  deviled crayfish 118
  dumplings 71
  frisée with sautéed shrimp
  mussels remoulade 74
  paella 111
  shrimp grilled in the shells 83
Seven-Minute Icing 63
Shallot and Artichoke Tarts 131
Shrimp
  grilled in the shells 83
  sautéed, with frisée 50
Smoked Salmon Roses 95
Soups
  consommé with herb dumplings
  fish 18
  fresh pea 20
  pistou 121
  roasted vegetable 21
  white gazpacho with grapes 108
Spicy Dipping Sauce 71
Spicy Fried Chicken 102
Spring Salad
  with Citrus Vinaigrette 46
Squash 136
Stars and Stripes Salad 103
Stocks
  chicken 20, 57
  fish 18

T

Tempering Chocolate 36
Tomatoes, herbed salad 47
Torta di Riso (rice torte) 83

V

Vanilla Buttercream 61
Veal, braised shanks 132
Vegetable Dumplings 71
Vegetable Hearts 31
Vintage Linens 29
Violet Nosegays 94

W

Warm Berry Compote 40
White Gazpacho with Grapes 108
White Sangria 108

Y

Yellow Tomato Vinaigrette 49

✳

If you have enjoyed reading and using The Best of Martha Stewart Living: Special Occasions *please join us as a subscriber to* Martha Stewart Living, *the magazine. Simply call toll-free 800-999-6518. The annual subscription rate is $24 for 10 issues.*